sycTESTS®

GW00858530

WHAT DO YOU DO IN THE

Midst

OF A *Suddenly?*

PAULA E. YORKER

xulon PRESS

Copyright © 2013 by Paula E. Yorker

What Do You Do in the Midst of a Suddenly?
by Paula E. Yorker

Printed in the United States of America

ISBN 9781628716115

All rights reserved solely by the author. The author guarantees all contents are original and do not infringe upon the legal rights of any other person or work. No part of this book may be reproduced in any form without expressed written permission of the author. The views expressed in this book are not necessarily those of the publisher.

All quotes, unless otherwise noted, are from THE MESSAGE: The Bible in Contemporary Language copyright © 2002 by Eugene Peterson. All rights reserved. (*The Message Bible Online*)

Scriptures marked NIV are taken from the HOLY BIBLE, NEW INTERNATIONAL VERSION. Copyright © 1973, 1978, 1984 by International Bible Society. Used by permission of Zondervan Publishing House. All rights reserved.

www.xulonpress.com

Dedication

To my Heavenly Father, God Almighty, if anyone knows and understands the pain, that one feels when loosing a child, that someone is you. Thank you for not allowing your emotions and the voice of others to get in the way of the purpose and the plan. Had you not remained focused in the midst of the pain I would be forever lost. Thank You Daddy~

As an only child, it is nice to know that you are not alone. Jesus Christ you are not just my Lord and Savior, but my elder brother and best friend. Thank you for not only having my back but for being my compassionate High Priest~ I Love You Forever!

Holy Spirit, thank you for upholding Al and I with your Grace and Strength as we continue our journey through this suddenly! I Love you! ~

<u>~I never knew how much love my heart could hold until someone called me mommy ~</u>

Sia Christine Yorker ~ your dad and I are so thankful to God for the 19 beautiful years and 11 months that we not only had with you but also for the lives that He allowed you to touch along the way and that are still being impacted. Thank You for Loving God, Loving People and Living Life! **"This Is Not The End Of The Story, It is Just The Beginning!"**

~This book is dedicated to every parent that has experienced the loss of a child~

Acknowledgments

To my handsome Boaz ~Thank you for loving Jesus Christ and for being the Priest and Prophet of our home. I'm so glad that we can still put on Frankie Beverly, Marvin Gaye, Ray Charles and Dance together, Laugh together and still enjoy life even in the midst of our Suddenly! I Love you Al (Josh) Yorker! God gave me His best when He gave me you!

To my spiritual parents~ Bishop Owen & Pastor Maggie McGregor- Berea South Africa and Apostle Mosy & Gloria Madugba-Port Harcourt Nigeria. Thank you for being a Godly example to me, Al and Sia. Thank you for your love and prayers throughout the years; for checking on us, holding us accountable and for making sure that we were **then** and are **now** still walking with Jesus Christ! We are forever grateful to God for placing you two special couples in our lives. I Love you with all of my heart! Your precious Paula ~

To my former pastors~ Darnell Hawkins & Sam Hinn, your heart of worship truly showed me how to enter into the presence of God and worship Him in spirit and in truth no matter the situation or who is around. I will be forever grateful for this impartation.

My dear sister Martha Munizzi, thank you for inviting me to the 2013 Viva De La Women Conference. I appreciate you keeping it real with the message about Alice in Wonderland, and allowing Holy Spirit to enter in which created an atmosphere for one to be totally free in "His Presence" Your Sista was really in need of that. You will never know the impact and healing that I received during the conference, which led me back to focusing **on** and **completing this book**.

Ms. Carmen May better known as mother Cookie, you are really an inspiration and one sent from heaven to help me every step of the way in completing this book. I could not have completed it without your untiring help. You were always there, even during the long hours, crying with me and encouraging me to go deeper into what I was trying to convey to the readers. Your help with formatting, grammar, and so much more was truly a blessing. I was in English class 101, 202, and 303 all over again. Who would have ever thought Memorial Day 2013 in the water at the beach would be our hook up and the rest is history. Thank you from the depths of my being. I Love you!

Randal (Bas), Nayabu and Jason Yorker~ Sons your dad and me are so grateful to God for your lives. Bas and Nayabu, thank you for coming to be with us immediately when you heard the news about your sister. Your presence made everything run so much smoother. We had so much fun, even in the midst! Carmen and Tokunbo Yorker, thank you for releasing your husbands to be with pops and I for those two weeks (I have the best daughter in laws in the world). Jason, we appreciate the time we had with you and Lil Diana in Virginia. Thanks for taking me and your dad out to dinner. It was precious.

~ Barbara and Jennifer ~ "True Friends" are like walls. Sometimes you lean on them, and sometimes it's good just knowing they are there. I Love You both~

Thanks to everyone who prayed for the completion of this book. Because of your love, prayers and encouragement, It is finished! To God Be the Glory!

Preface

Why this Title?

*E*ven though the term suddenly sounds strange to some, and it has even been suggested that I change the title, this is the title the Lord Jesus Christ placed within my heart. They are not my words but His.

I pray that the words on each page of this book come alive in your heart, and that Holy Spirit will bring healing to you as you confront your own life "suddenlies."

I was truly touched and blessed while reading your book.

The presence of God permeates through the pages. I could feel your hurts, pain and faith in the goodness of God. Continue to be sensitive to the Holy Spirit. Your faith and zeal is an inspiration to every person that comes in contact with you.

In this book Paula Yorker is bearing her soul so that all can see the hurt, tears, turmoil, pain and comfort received from the Holy Spirit as she was carried through the worst kind of "suddenly" that could hit her house and family.

Life happens to every one. Bad things happen to good people. This book will help to deal with things that are out of our control.

I would highly recommend every person get a copy of this book, especially those that have lost a loved one and those that are struggling to come to terms with the death of a child. This book is "a must have" for people involved in grief counseling.

Bishop Owen McGregor
Mount Calvary Pentecostal Church

Table of Contents

I

What Do You Do in the Midst of a Suddenly?

$\mathcal{A}$s individuals, we have a tendency to try to control situations, things, and people. We even believe that we are in charge of our destiny, and the turns and curves that occur along the journey. We have our day planned from A-Z, everything so well organized. Will meet Lisa at 8:45 a.m. for breakfast, meeting at 10:30 a.m., hair appointment at 12:30 p.m., pick kids up from school by 3:00 p.m., etc. But what about the curve balls—the suddenlies—along the way? Like baseball players, we don't always see the curve balls coming.

You're out on the ball field, positioned to move the way you're accustomed to moving; you know the way you've planned. The batter is up, swings the bat, hits the ball, and all of a sudden the ball goes in a different direction than you thought, totally catching you off guard, messing up the entire play. Depending on how you respond, it can mess up your disposition, your life, and even your destiny.

A suddenly is something that one is not in control of or has the time to prepare for. You don't see it coming. It catches you totally off guard. It comes out of the blue, swiftly or even abruptly. I would have to say it's almost like a tornado which can turn your life upside down and leave you in a whirlwind! Some people actually panic and freak out when things don't go as planned. Did you know that a suddenly can cause some people to become angry, bitter, anxious, fretful, unforgiving, and resentful toward friends, loved ones, and even God?

The truth is, no matter how much you and I think we are in control, have our day and our lives all planned and in order, a suddenly will take place from time to time and change all of that. The Bible says in Proverbs 19:21, "There are many plans in the heart of a man, but only the plans of God shall prosper (prevail)." It's imperative that you and I realize that how we respond to a suddenly or an unexpected situation will determine the outcomes that the suddenly will have on our lives; even whether we survive or perish.

September 11, 2001

I'm reminded of the suddenly that took place on September 11, 2001, which shook the entire world. Two planes were flown into the towers of the World Trade Center in New York City, a third plane hit the Pentagon just outside Washington, D.C., and the fourth plane crashed in a field in Pennsylvania. Over

3,000 people were killed during the attacks, including more than 400 police officers and firefighters.

My dear friends Dennis and Donna Vauck from Houston, Texas, lost a loved one when the third plane crashed into the Pentagon just outside Washington, D.C. Dennis's brother, Ron was a Lieutenant Commander on watch at the Pentagon during the time of plane crash. When the family received the news about the episode, they gathered together and began to pray, believing that Ron was alive and well. However, almost one week later, the family watched a colonel walk up the walkway of the Vauck's home to bring the terrible news of the death of their loved one, Ron.

Ron's wife never thought the morning Ron left to go to work would be the last time she would ever see him. This was a suddenly, something this family and many others had no control over. But even in the midst of the suddenly something good came, little Megan, Ron's daughter was born two months later.

January 12, 2010

Another incident that comes to mind is the earth-quake that took place Tuesday, January 12, 2010 in Haiti near the town of Leogane, approximately sixteen miles west of Port-au-Prince, Haiti's capital. There were approximately three million people affected by the suddenly of this quake. An estimated 316,000 people died, 300,000 were injured, and over 1,000,000 were left homeless.

In November of 2012, two years after the earthquake, my husband and I had the opportunity to visit Danita's Children, an Orphanage in Quanaminthe, Haiti. This was a life changing experience. There we met fifteen year old Katiana who was at home sitting at the kitchen table doing her homework when the earthquake hit Port-au-Prince, Haiti.

A loud noise like a roaring train was heard and the house collapsed about her causing her to lose one of her arms. Katiana had lost her mother due to illness prior to the earthquake. Her dad went missing and she later found out that he had been killed in the earthquake.

In July of 2013 I revisited Danita's Children with a five member mission team. With us was twenty-two year old Janice from our church who also experienced a dramatic suddenly in her life in 2010 when she lost her arm and almost lost her life while riding in a car with some friends under the influence of alcohol. It was amazing how these suddenlies in these two young ladies' lives from different parts of the world created almost an instant connection.

Suddenlies

We all have suddenlies that we will have to walk through in life! Someone reading this book right now is walking through a situation that almost knocked the very wind out of you. This situation just occurred out of nowhere, you didn't see it coming. As a matter of fact you thought things were improving until you visited your family doctor for your yearly check-up.

You went in happy. However, you left the doctor's office dismayed by the shocking news of being diagnosed with an incurable disease.

All parents desire the best for their children. You watch them grow, attend sport activities, school plays, and look forward to the day when little Johnny or Sabrina graduates from high school and gets accepted at the finest University or College. We never anticipate those dreams being shattered by the news of that sixteen-year-old daughter, the one that you hoped would far succeed you by attending college and becoming a productive citizen in society, is now pregnant and has decided to drop out of High School to live with Malcolm and his mother who sells drugs.

What about the job that you gave your all to, spent most of your time, and gave all of your energy to hoping to get the promotion? In the meantime your wife and children received the short end of the stick because you were too busy chasing after destiny. You were depending on man to make things happen instead of God, just to find out after all that chasing, the company is downsizing and guess *who's next to be laid off*? You! That sounds like a **suddenly**!

Let's say you receive a phone call from one of your children who is away at college. He is coming home for Thanksgiving and asks permission to bring one of their friends home for the holiday break.

You are so excited that Michael has met some nice friends at school and wants to bring one home for the holiday to meet the family. Without a second thought your response is, "Yes! Honey, that would be great! I've been praying that God would place good friends in your path."

The day has finally arrived for their visit, the doorbell rings, you run to the door with excitement, answer the door, greet your son with a big hug and kiss on cheek, and welcome his guest. As the day goes on you begin to notice some strange behavior going on between Michael and Mark. You don't want to say anything right away, so you think to yourself that you will keep your other eye open; just sit back and observe closely.

When you enter the living room you notice how closely Michael and Mark are sitting, the way they look at one another as they chat. Immediately, you go to your bedroom and begin to pray. "Lord, what is going on here. I know this can't be what I think it is!" A part of you wants to stay in the bedroom, and the other part is praying that what you are sensing is untrue. All of a sudden there is a knock on your bedroom door. It's Michael asking if he can come in. You try to regain your composure before he enters the room.

Michael opens the door, looks at your face, and knows immediately something is wrong. You ask him to close the door and sit next to you on the bed. With the palm of your hands sweating and your heart pounding, you look him in his eyes as you begin to ask the question that you dread hearing the answer to. "Michael, are you living a homosexual lifestyle?" With tears running down his face Michael looks you in your eyes and says, "Yes, Mommy, I am a homosexual. Mommy, I never meant to hurt you and didn't really know how to tell you." At that moment your heart drops as you hear his response. You feel as if you were hit by a semi-truck. This is your baby, the one you rocked to sleep at night, played catch with, now twenty years of age. Your little Michael tells you that he's gay.

Michael comes from a good godly home. He's a very intelligent and respectful handsome young man. All the girls were head over heels with him and believe it or not, he really loves Jesus! The news literally knocks the very wind out of you. You sit there devastated, with a thousand thoughts racing through your mind. Where did we go wrong? How come I didn't see the signs? What signs, there were no signs at all? He dated girls. Oh my goodness, what will we tell the family?

Perhaps your suddenly didn't occur with a Michael and Mark coming home from college during Thanksgiving break, but it could have been a Patty and Leola! No matter the gender, it's still considered to be a **suddenly**!

Life is full of suddenlies! You come home from work and find your spouse on the computer not working on a project but looking at pornography. He becomes very defensive, catches an attitude with you for exposing his little secret, tries to flip the script, and blame you for not meeting his needs.

Later you find out that he's hooked and has no intention of stopping, doesn't want counseling, and can't understand why you're so hurt, angry, and disappointed about his addiction, and why you don't want him to touch you. This is the man that you were so in love with, have children with, planned to spend the rest of your life with, only to have your dreams ruined by a suddenly that you never saw coming.

What about the time that you were molested by your neighbor, cousin, uncle, auntie, brother, step dad, biological dad or perhaps all of the above starting at the age of five or six? You were threatened that if you told anyone, you and your family would be hurt. When you finally gained the courage to speak up, no one would listen to you. They thought you were lying, just trying to cause problems or get attention. So you held on to this pain and trauma for years, thinking that it would eventually go away. Now you have found out that the suddenly that you tried to fix by blocking it out is now tormenting you at the age of twenty-five or forty-two, causing moments of explosive behavior, fits of rage, low self-esteem, and keeping you from enjoying true intimacy with your spouse because you always see the perpetrator's face. This suddenly that you've been holding onto has held you hostage for years and robbed you of being an effective husband, wife, mother, brother, sister, aunt, uncle, cousin or even friend.

Your parents were hard working citizens, became very successful and decided to retire, travel, and enjoy life. Everything was going great; they were relaxing in the sun, traveling, sewing, golfing, etc. However, slowly your dad begins to notice that your mom is forgetting things such as doctor's appointments which she never forgets or that she's preparing lunch for the second time when she and dad just finished eating lunch. She's even forgetting the names of her grandchildren or asking the same questions that she asked five minutes ago. To top it all off, this morning your mom woke up at 3 a.m. on a Thursday morning, insisting that it's 7:00 a.m. Sunday morning. She gets fully dressed, prepares breakfast, and begins to head out the door for church before she is stopped by your father. Luckily the smell of the burnt bacon woke him up. This about does it for your dad.

He calls you and your siblings, concerned, frustrated, and fearful that something terrible is happening to his best friend. You try to calm him by assuring him that mom is okay, probably a little tired. To put him at ease you tell him that you and your siblings will fly into town over the weekend for a week to spend some time with him and mom. During the visit, you and your siblings notice that mom's behavior is a little different.

Sometimes during conversations she forgets your names or mixes up the names of her loved ones, calling Sharon by your cousin's name. The only name she hasn't been confused about was your brother Tyler. She managed to play it off during the early part of the visit, but towards that latter part of the week you couldn't help but notice it was hap-pening quite often. Throughout the course of the day, conversations with your mom would always revert back to her childhood. Then she would have a hard time recalling prior conversations or events from ten minutes ago or yesterday. You find that she becomes very agitated when she is told, "Mom, you just said that."

When you ask her why she was repeating herself or talking about childhood events especially when that was not the topic of conversation, she becomes quite hostile with her choice of words and the tone of voice which is totally out of her character. You remember your mom as always very pleasant, sweet, soft spoken yet stern when needed. You know something is definitely wrong and decide to contact your mother's doctor. After meeting with her doctor to further discuss her behavior, he decides to run a series of tests which show a slow decline in memory, thinking, and reasoning skills. At the end of the day your mom, your father's best friend has been diagnosed with a brain disease called Alzheimer's/dementia. That's an unexpected suddenly that is happening far too often in many families today.

Perhaps after being married for twenty-eight years you find out your spouse is having an affair with someone that you trusted which happens to not only be a friend but a family member, pretty deep, huh? But it happens! I know someone reading this is saying, it is one thing to have an affair, but with a family member, that's a whole different story! This is a suddenly that we encounter today at all levels of the socioeconomic ladder, in all communities, in all races and people of all faiths, and has been so easily accepted.

Suddenlies! You and your family were covenant members at a local church for an extended period of time. Not only did your children grow up there, you watched other children grow up in the same church. This was a thriving place of worship within the community which always looked for ways to help others inside the house of God as well as in the community. Several years down the road, you noticed things began to change, you couldn't put your finger on it, you just knew within your heart there was a shift in gears, not forward but backward.

Although you served as a leader in the house, you never really hung out with the inner circle after church. You did Wednesdays and Sundays together, which was nice. However, it didn't allow for an extended time of fellowship because everyone was always busy serving. Nevertheless, everyone felt the love towards each other, and would often speak the phrase, "I love you."

You'd say, "See you next Wednesday" or "Be there on Sunday the Lord willing," then you got in your car and drove off until the next gathering. Suddenly you receive a telephone call informing you of an emergency church meeting. With much anticipation you wondered to yourself on the way to the meeting, what's so urgent? The church is packed inside, more attendees showed up for this church meeting than Sunday morning worship! The board members walk to the front of the church to address the congregation with news that devastates the entire church. Pastor Jones was being asked to resign for an extended period of time due to having an extramarital affair with someone from the church for several years. Or perhaps it was Father Riley who was called before the Bishop or even worse, pedophilia. At any rate, the sound of the entire church is a deep inhale like the sound of one gasping for breath.

As you sat there heartbroken, you began to look around the sanctuary to capture the facial expressions of some of the congregants. Some are crying, some shaking as if they are having a nervous breakdown, some in a state of shock, some look empty, and others are very quiet. You began thinking, WOW! This is the pastor (the man or woman) that you loved, trusted, respected, and sat under Sunday after Sunday for years. He baptized your children, married your son, prophesied and prayed over your children, provided marriage counseling for you and your wife, visited your grandmother while she was sick in the hospital, and led her to the Lord before she passed.

There's a part of you that actually feels sorry and compassionate towards him (not the sin) because you know in your heart he isn't a bad person, he has a good heart. You can't even begin to imagine what his precious family must be going through or the other family involved for that matter. But on the other hand you realize that you are angry, disappointed, and let down. You looked up to Pastor Jones. As a matter of fact, he was like a father to you. You would have given your life for Pastor Jones and to make it even worse, these were the very things he preached against. He deceived you. You may never trust another pastor again! They are all hypocrites! Your thoughts are that there is no honesty in the House of God! You may not want to go to church anymore! Why? Because of this suddenly! You're hurt; he hurt you bad!

God knows about the whirlwind that you have just been hit with. However, if you would just hold on to God and keep your heart pure, God will give you His grace to walk in and through the suddenly that you have been hit with. You may be thinking, yeah, well, that's easy for you to say, you're not in my situation. You know what? You're absolutely correct, but remember what I mentioned earlier everyone will encounter a suddenly in life. No one is exempt and you don't get to pick and choose your suddenly.

My Suddenly

I stated earlier that a suddenly is something that one is not in control of or has time to prepare for. You don't see it coming. It catches you totally off guard. My suddenly began Friday, June 17, 2011. The night before our suddenly, Sia our daughter had an early shift at Ross Department store after school, which allowed her to get home before 5:30 p.m. Earlier during the week I had promised my husband that I would serve with him and the team at the Volusia County Prison. Sia arrived home from work shortly after I did. It was nice seeing her early since her normal arrival time after work would be around 10 p.m. Although Sia had made plans to hang out with some friends that evening, for some reason I was torn between the prison or staying home with her, even though she had plans to go out. Prior to our leaving for the prison, she was trying to select her outfit to wear and studying for a test on Monday at Seminole State College. According to the weather forecast there was heavy rain headed our way.

I tried to talk her out of going, but her response was, "Mom we will be fine."

Her dad and I prayed over her, anointed her with olive oil, and kissed her before heading out. All of Sia's friends knew they could never leave our house without being prayed for.

Sometimes they would say, "Mom, you forgot to pray for us."

On the way to the prison the rain began to come down very hard. Inside my heart I had this feeling as if I needed to be home with Sia. We arrived at the Volusia County Prison, Male Division. My husband Al who I also call Josh, Bob Andrews, and I went to the pod we were assigned to, began to pray over the room, and retrieved the Bibles from the shelf in the closet to have them readily available for the men once they entered the class room.

While waiting for the men, we could hear the rain coming down very hard. I couldn't shake the feeling of my needing to be home with Sia. Bob began to pray that Sia and her friends wouldn't go out because of the rain. A couple seconds later, the Correctional Officer came into the classroom to inform us that the prison had to cancel the ministry time due to the power outage on the other side of the facility. We had to leave immediately. All I could say was, "Thank You, Jesus!"

I immediately gathered my belongings and said, "Come on Honey, we have to go; I need to get home to Sia before she leaves."

There was such urgency within my heart. As we proceeded out of the facility to the car, the rain was heavy with hail. Al and I got in the car, buckled up, and headed home. I asked him if he could drive faster,

I just needed to get home before Sia left. I began to pray in my heavenly language. I turned the radio on which at that moment had a sudden interruption from the weather service forecasting a tornado watch for Volusia County and surrounding area. I asked my husband if he could drive even faster. Now this is something I would never ask him to do. It would be the opposite, "Honey, slow down."

Al responded by saying, "Honey, it's a tornado watch, we're driving in a bad storm. You of all people want me to drive faster!"

I said, "Josh, I can't explain it, I just need to get home to Sia before she leaves. I know this is going to sound weird, but I feel as if this is my last night with her. I can't explain it."

I had tears running down my face. We finally arrived home, her car was still in the driveway! All I could say was, "Thank You, Jesus!" I immediately opened the car door and ran out in the rain straight to the front door. I opened the front door and headed straight for her room, only to find her in the bathroom putting last minute touches on her hair.

I remember running to her, grabbing her and kissing Sia saying "I'm so glad that you are still here! I love you, I'm so glad that I had a chance to see you before you left!"

She looked at me and said, "Mom! I love you, too. What's wrong with you? Why are you acting as if something is wrong?"

I just held her and told her that I loved her and that I was glad that we got home before she left. I also explained to her the situation that took place at the prison due to the storm and how the three of us (her dad, Mr. Bob, and I) came into agreement with all of heaven as Mr. Bob prayed that you would not go out tonight due to the storm.

She smiled and said, "Um Huh! Okay, Mr. Bob, you and dad and all of heaven, I thought you all were on my side."

I told her that we were! "I thought you knew that girl!"

Sia looked at me and said, "Ma!"

Sia, Josh, and I began to laugh! I went to shower, put on pajamas, and began to pop some popcorn on the stove to prepare for a movie. A few moments later, Sia came out of her room with this look of disappointment on her face. I asked what was wrong. Sia said that she'd just received a phone call from Christina (one of her best friends) to inform Sia that although it had stopped raining, her aunt would not allow her to go out due to the storm. I told her that God knows everything. Perhaps the three of us were to have family night tonight and watch a movie together. For those of you who have a nineteen year old, you know they do not want to hear that (especially if it was not their suggestion). At the age of nineteen, I had my own apartment, was working full time, and attending college in the evenings, so you know I had other plans on a Friday night. Can I keep it real!

Sia went in her room and began to work on some homework. Shortly after, I went in her room and rubbed her back and told her not to be upset with Christina.

"I'm sure Christina was disappointed as well, but the truth of the matter is neither one of you are grown. As upset as you both may be, Christina has to respect her aunt's decision, God honors that! He honors respect."

I leaned over to kiss her forehead, and as I walked out of her room she said, "Mom, I know, I know God honors her respecting her aunt's decision."

Five minutes later, the three of us, including little Biscuit (our Shih Tzu dog) were lounging in the family room eating popcorn with black pepper and watching a movie.

Saturday morning June 18, 2011, the house was quiet, my husband was still asleep, which I thought was glorious, since he's always the first to rise; especially on Saturday mornings to prepare his famous buttermilk pancakes with "Alaga Syrup" for the family. As I watched him resting so peacefully, I began to rehearse in my mind the things that were on my schedule for the day. You know like go to the gym, stop by the bank, rush home to shower, and prepare for prison ministry with the male juveniles at the 33rd Street jail, etc. As I tiptoed around the room, got dressed, and quietly closed the bedroom door trying not to awaken Al, I headed to the kitchen to fix a cup of tea and softly whispered, "Thank you, Father Sia has an opportunity to sleep in today, no school, and she doesn't have to go to work until later." As I began to sip tea, I heard a loud sound, coming from the area of the laundry room. I said to myself, "What in the world was that?"

As I proceeded towards the laundry room, I stopped and said to myself, *Um huh! Sia's up and has a little attitude because she had to get up a little early to wash those clothes that I asked her to wash last night.* Then I said to myself, *You know what; I'm not going there this morning!* (I know many of you can relate to that statement and have perhaps used it at one time or another).

So I turned around and went to the living room to sit down to have my devotion before leaving for the gym. Just before my bottom hit the chair, I heard Holy Spirit whisper go get your towel! I said, "My towel. Oh thank You, Holy Spirit, you are such a gentleman." As I headed to the laundry room which required me to go through Sia's bathroom, I found her lying on the bathroom floor almost unconscious with a towel under her head and her feet towards the toilet seat. I got down on my knees, called her name several times, and began to gently shake her a few times before she responded.

I asked her if she'd fallen and she whispered very softly, "No Mommy, it's my head, I put the towel under my head and laid down, it's my head!"

Immediately I woke my husband and told him to call the ambulance, "It's her head baby, Sia's on the bathroom floor!"

I then realized that Sia had heard me in the kitchen, was too weak to call out so with all of her strength, she'd lifted up the toilet seat with her feet allowing it to slam down trying to get my attention for help. I sat on the bathroom floor rubbing her face. My husband and I prayed over her as we waited for the ambulance to arrive. I felt a little like the song written by Marvin Gaye, "What's Going On, Tell Me What's Going On!" The paramedics arrived, took her vitals, asked her some questions which she responded to, slid her on the stretcher, started an IV, and carried her to the ambulance. I rode with the paramedics as they headed to the hospital with my baby. Although she was a little weak, Sia and I talked and smiled along the way.

As a matter of fact she said to me, "Mommy, I have to go to work later."

My husband and I always taught Sia that a person is only as good as their word. If you can't do something, let people know, don't leave them hanging, even if they get mad. At the end of the day that person will respect you for being honest. I thank God for Sia's heart, commitment, accountability, and faithfulness. If she gave her word to do something, you could take it to the bank. Her word was always her bond! If she couldn't do something she would let you know upfront.

But honestly at that moment, my response was, "Girl, it's not that important, we will deal with the job later. The most important thing at this moment is finding out what's going on with you!"

As the on-call chaplain of the very hospital we were headed to, I'd traveled to the hospital many times in the middle of the night to pray for patients who may be in a life or death situation, comfort loved ones, etc. I was very aware of the length of time it took one to travel from my home to the hospital, approximately twelve minutes driving the designated speed limit.

However, the morning of June 18, 2011, the ride seemed as if it lasted forever. After what seemed like a long scenic route drive, we finally arrived at the hospital. Sia was placed in a room within the emergency room. The nurse came in immediately to care for Sia. After the nurse left, Sia and I began to chat a bit. She seemed very weak and her little fingers were a little limp.

As I stood over her I said, "Sia, are you okay, baby? Mommy's trying to understand all of this."

Her response very softly was, "Mommy, it's my head!"

I said "Okay, let's pray!"

I began to pray over her and then I sat down.

She said, "Mommy, Biscuit."

I said. "Sia, he's at home."

She said, "No, Mommy, Biscuit found me."

"He found you!"

"Yes Mommy, in the bathroom," she said.

I said, "Oh, so that's where Biscuit went! What did he do?"

She smiled and said, "He licked me."

I said, "Oh that is so sweet!"

At that moment, my husband arrived and began to chat with her. He always called Sia his Boom Boom!

"How's daddy's Boom Boom doing?"

She whispered, "I'm okay."

Moments later my husband noticed that Sia was having a seizure, her hands and arms became flexed and rigid, and one side of her face was flaccid. A retired nurse, I'm glad that my husband was there and able to recognize what was happening. I always thought that signs of seizures were when one's tongue curled up in one's mouth. However, I have since learned there are various types of seizures with many manifestations.

Josh and I immediately called for the nursing staff, they came in and began to work on Sia and then escorted her to X-ray for a CAT scan. Josh and I just stood there looking at each other, wondering if this was really happening! We held each other tightly and continued to pray. While waiting for the results, we made a few calls to family and friends. Mrs. Netta and Rhonda dropped everything and immediately came to the hospital. (Thank You for being there for our Sia).

As Sia returned from the X-Ray, Josh over-heard the doctor comment that Sia was going to be transferred to Halifax hospital. When he asked the doctor why, the doctor informed us that the CAT Scan showed some bleeding on the outside of the right side of the brain. The doctor wanted to know if Sia had a fall or hit her head. We told her no, if Sia would have fallen or hit her head, trust us, she would have told us.

The doctor advised us that Sia would have to be air lifted to Daytona or Orlando hospital to have a neurologist monitor her since this particular hospital didn't specialize in neurosurgery. My husband and I chose Halifax Hospital in Daytona Beach, Florida.

One thing that I learned during this suddenly is that whenever you have emergency health issues, instead of going to the closest community hospital, make sure that you go to the closest hospital that specializes in your physical need. For example; if you're having chest pains, heart problems, go to the closest hospital that has a cardiologist on staff. This may help to prolong your life and prevent you from wasting time. When it's a matter of life and death, every moment counts!

At this time Sia was lying on the bed, with a breathing mask over her face.

I bent over and whispered in her ear, "Sia did you fall or hit your head?"

She whispered very weakly, "No Mommy!"

I told Sia that she was going to be flown by helicopter to Halifax so that a neurologist could monitor her, and that I couldn't be in the helicopter with her, but Daddy and I would meet her there. I asked her to squeeze my hand if she could hear me and she did!

I also told her not to worry, "Just call on the name of Jesus baby!"

I told her how much I loved her and kissed her cheek. She sat up for a moment, as if she was trying to tell me something, she even tried to take the mask off her face. Her dad and I told her to relax and try to stay calm. Everything was going to be okay!

"Jesus is with you and He will be with you in the helicopter," I said as my husband and I both kissed her cheek, told her that we loved her, and helped her lay back down.

Once the helicopter arrived, I whispered in her ear, "Dad and I are heading over to the hospital. Sia, if you can't think of anything else to say, just say

JESUS! JESUS! JESUS! He can hear you! Squeeze mommy's hand if you can hear me!"

She squeezed my hand! Josh, Rhonda and I headed for Halifax hospital, not knowing what was to come. After arriving at Halifax, the first face we saw was Mother Pauline McDowell. We were so surprised that she arrived before us since she lived further away. We were so thankful that she loved us enough to be there for our Sia. We thank her from the depth of our hearts for demonstrating the love of a mother, and the meaning of true friendship during our suddenly.

Josh and I went to the desk to ask which room Sia Yorker was in. To our surprise, we were informed that Sia had been taken into surgery immediately upon arrival!

We looked at each other and said, "Surgery! No one told us she was going to have surgery, we thought that she was going to be monitored."

The receptionist gave us directions to the waiting room and told us the doctor would come out to speak with us just as soon as the surgery was finished. Rhonda, Mother McDowell, my husband, and I took off walking and running as fast as we could.

Mother McDowell took off her shoes so that she could move quickly, we all knew this was urgent and we had no time to waste.

I prayed, "Lord, if my baby had to have surgery, let her surgeon be a Christian, a man or woman of God and of faith!"

Once we arrived at the surgical waiting room, the only thing that I knew to do was to fall to my knees with tears rolling down my face and worship my Lord, Savior, and King.

I said, "Here I am to Worship, here I am to bow down, here I am to say that you are my God, You are all together lovely, all together wonderful to me. I'll never know how much it cost to see my sins upon that cross, so here I am to worship!"

There are times throughout life when situations occur that can be extremely devastating. That's the time we can't be concerned about who's around us, what others will think or even how our response looks to others. I didn't care how I looked or who was staring at me. I was in a desperate state and I knew no one could help my baby but Jesus Christ! I also knew that I needed to stay focused so that I could hear clearly from my Lord and not allow my emotions or the voice and opinions of others to overtake me! The songs continued to flow from my heart and out of my mouth as I stayed in that position on the floor! Songs such as, "Hallelujah! Hallelujah! Hallelujah! Lord I Love you! Lord I Love You! Lord I Trust You! Lord I Trust You!" And then, "What A Friend We Have In Jesus!"

Then I sang from my heart, "My life is not my own, to you do I belong, I give myself, I give myself to you, I give myself away, so you can use me! Sia's life is not her own, to you she does belong, she gives herself away so you can use her!" The last three songs I remember singing were, "It Is Well with My Soul," "As The Deer Pants For The Water," and "What A Mighty God We Serve!" As I worshipped Father in spirit and truth, no one and nothing else mattered. It was as if it were just He and me.

As we continued to wait for the doctor, the four of us held hands believing God for a miracle. During the wait, my husband and I made a few phone calls to our three sons, Bass, Nayabu, and Jason; my sister-in-law Maxie; my two uncles, Donald and Curtis; and other family members. We also called Pastor Sam and a few friends.

I remember calling my supervisor, Jordan Heaps, telling him about the situation concerning Sia, and that I didn't know when I would be returning to work. You could tell that he was in a state of shock hearing the news about Sia. She had visited me at work just recently. Jordan just saw me at work on Friday. As a matter of fact, on my way out I stopped by his office to tell him to have a nice weekend! Now here it was Saturday morning and he received a suddenly phone call concerning Sia. You and I never know what the next moment will bring.

Jordan's response was, "Paula, we will pray for her, and I will pass this information on to our church to pray for Sia as well. I'm so sorry Paula, I can't believe this! Call me if you need anything and take as much time as you need!"

I said, "Thanks Jordan, I will keep you posted! Thanks for your prayers."

By this time, the doctor came to the surgical waiting room and asked for Mr. and Mrs. Yorker, my my husband and I replied,

"Yes, we are Mr. and Mrs. Yorker."

"Hello, I'm Dr. Venus, Sia's surgeon."

Our immediate response was, "How is she?"

"Sia had what we call an Acute Brain Hemorrhage, some bleeding on the outside of the right side of her brain, which caused a small shift in the brain due to the pressure from the bleeding and she's in a coma."

My husband and I looked at one another and began to weep.

Josh told the doctor, "Do whatever it takes to ensure Sia is provided with the best of care!"

I knew my husband meant well, and I will always love and respect him for not only taking excellent care of his family, but also for covering us spiritually, physically, emotionally, and financially. But at this moment, I really understood the saying, "There are some things in life that 'whatever it takes' isn't enough, and there are some things money just can't buy!"

II

In the Midst of Your Suddenly, Take Your Eyes Off Your Situation!

*T*stood there thinking about so many things such as my baby being all alone after having serious surgery and me not being able to hold her. I wondered what was going on in her mind, what was she thinking about, did she feel alone, was she in pain, was she wondering where her dad and I were? So many thoughts raced through my mind. I even began to reminisce about the night before the suddenly.

Sia, her dad, Biscuit, and I were home eating pop-corn and watching a movie together. Not that it was Sia's first option on a Friday night, though. However, due to a tornado watch, she and three of her close friends cancelled their outing for that evening. Sia was a little disappointed because she hadn't visited with her buddies in a while with her busy college classes and work schedule. She missed her friends.

Her dad and I missed her as well and we were glad to have this time with her. Normally on a Friday night Sia had to work late. We were very proud of Sia for staying on top of her grades and working full time. We could also see that she was growing up and becoming an independent responsible young lady.

As I reminisced about Friday night thanking God for the movie time, I began rubbing my forehead thinking to myself, "Is this for real or what!"

We were trying to grasp all that Dr. Venus said in such a short period of time. It was almost as if it were a dream; I mean everything happened so quickly. I'm sure there were a million thoughts rushing through Josh's mind as well. Yet in the midst of everything, I can't explain it, but I still felt this calmness and peace!

I remember whispering, "Jesus, I trust You! I don't understand it all, but one thing I know is that I trust You!"

I walked off by myself for a few minutes trying to gather my thoughts and put things in perspective as much as I could. I realized at this point, I needed to encourage myself.

I whispered these words, "Jesus, I'm not going to take my eyes off of You. I refuse to allow the devil to get the victory!"

I looked up towards heaven and I began to think about Sia. She wouldn't want me to be sad right now. What would Sia want me to do at this very moment?

I thought to myself, "Perhaps there's someone here that needs Jesus or prayer. God be glorified!"

As I scoped out the area, I saw a young man around the age of eleven or twelve sitting in the chair near the surgical room with a book. I went over to him, and introduced myself. I asked him his name and began to chat with Mark about school, his favorite subjects, and if he knew anything about Jesus Christ.

Mark told me that he used to go to church with his family, but they didn't go much anymore. He shared how much he enjoyed going to church and some of the things that he learned. I told Mark that Jesus Christ loved him very much and that he had a great plan for his life. I asked if he'd ever invited Jesus Christ to live inside of his heart. Mark said yes, but he didn't feel as if Jesus was still there because he didn't talk to Jesus much and hadn't attended church in a long time.

I looked in Mark's eyes and asked him, "Would you like to invite Jesus Christ to live inside of your heart again, this time forever!

Mark's little eyes lit up with such excitement as he responded, "Would I!"

I get teary eyes every time I think of our conversation. Mark had such innocence and purity of heart. Lord, please help me to always desire and love you as a child with an innocent and pure heart. I'm reminded of Mark 10:14-16.

The people brought children to Jesus, hoping he might touch them. The disciples shooed them off. But Jesus was irate and let them know it: "Don't push these children away. Don't ever get between them and me. These children are at the very center of life in the kingdom. Mark this: Unless you accept God's

Kingdom in the simplicity of a child, you'll never get in." Then, gathering the children up in His arms, he laid his hands of blessing on them. (MSG)

After explaining to Mark what it meant to invite Jesus Christ to live inside of his heart, I assured him that Jesus would be delighted to be his friend and live in his heart forever. Then I showed him John 3:16 in the Bible and asked him to read it aloud for himself!

Mark and I prayed together, and he accepted Jesus Christ as His Lord and Savior! We also prayed that he and his family would start attending church together.

With a puzzled look on his face, Mark looked up at me and asked, "Why are you at the hospital?"

I took a deep breath and began to tell him about Sia. He asked me if Sia was going to be alright.

I smiled with tears in my eyes and told Mark, "The same Jesus that we just prayed to and invited to live in your heart is the same Jesus that is taking good care of Sia right now!"

I asked Mark if he would like to pray to Jesus for Sia and he responded, "Yes!"

Mark and I held hands as we prayed for my Sia. I gave him a hug, thanked him, and asked him to promise Jesus and Sia that he would live for Jesus all the days of his life!

He said, "I promise Jesus and Sia!"

Soon after we finished, a lady came up to him, and he said, "This is my mom."

I said hello to her and told her that she had a very nice son, that we had been talking about church and

Jesus Christ, and that he had invited Jesus Christ to live in his heart.

She smiled and said, "Thank you so much for talking with him!"

I told her that I was waiting to visit with my daughter who just had surgery. His mom asked me the person's name that I was waiting for. When I told her Sia Yorker, her eyes became big as she informed me that she was the one who had met Sia upon her arrival in the helicopter and had prepared her for surgery.

I said, "You took care of my Sia when she arrived!"

I smiled and thanked her for being there for our Sia, and this precious mother in return thanked me for being there for her son.

At that moment all I could do was look up towards heaven and smile, thanking my Lord for orchestrating my time with this family. During my conversation with Mark, I was reminded by God of how so many children cry out for Him daily, but as adults, sometimes we're not listening. I can't begin to tell you the importance of raising your child in a godly home. Allowing the person of Jesus Christ to be seen in your life consistently on a daily basis as a way of life and fellowshipping together as a family at a local church that love God, love people, and live life is so vital!

I know that there are people that used to attend church (the building) but for whatever reasons, they've stopped going. Maybe it's because of their work schedule or maybe they were hurt in the church. Maybe they got caught up in sin and felt as if they were not worthy. The truth of the matter is that none of us that attend the building is worthy. It's only because of the precious blood of Jesus Christ that any of us are able to have fellowship with Father.

After hugging little Mark I headed back to the surgical waiting room when I noticed an elderly woman sitting in the waiting room looking as if she was a little distraught. I went over and sat next to her and asked if she was okay. She informed me that her husband was having open heart surgery and she was a little nervous. It was also their forty-second wedding anniversary. I asked her if I could pray for her and her husband.

She smiled and said, "Oh yes, please."

I prayed for the both of them and gave her a hug. I asked her if she and her husband were Christians, her response was yes!

She asked me who I was waiting for and I told her about our Sia!

She said, "Oh! I'm sorry!"

I told her, "It's okay, God is with her!"

She began to pray for Sia right on the spot. I thanked her so much for her prayer.

She then looked at me and asked, "How can you be so calm and peaceful, praying for other people's needs when your child is going through something?"

I looked at her with tears in my eyes and said, "God is so loving and kind, He knew how you were feeling and He wanted you to know that He loves you and your husband just as much as He loves me and my Sia! Happy Anniversary!"

She just started crying and whispered, "Thank You!"

I said, "No, thank Jesus! He's worthy!"

At this time our former pastor, Sam Hinn arrived. Al and I filled him in as to Sia's status. Rhonda's husband Carl and son Parris arrived shortly after Pastor Sam. We all chatted for a short time. Then Dr. Venus came out to escort us to the surgical room to see Sia. Not knowing what to really expect, I took a deep breath as we walked through the double doors and over to Sia's bed.

As I'm sitting at my dining room table typing the words on the computer to complete this book, I can see it as if it was only yesterday. Sia was laying there so peaceful as if she was in a deep sleep, resting, recuperating with tubes in her mouth, bandage wrappings around her head, and all sorts of machines hooked up to her. I leaned over and kissed Sia on her cheeks and rubbed her face. My husband began to weep loudly as he talked with her and kissed his Boom-Boom. Everyone took turns giving her a kiss on her cheek and encouraging her. We all held hands as Pastor Sam led the prayer. Then we shifted from prayer into all of us singing worship songs unto the Lord around Sia's bedside. In spite of all that I saw in the natural, there was such a peace within my heart!

The nurse informed us that Sia would be transferred momentarily to her room. We all shared a few words with Sia and headed out to the waiting room. Before leaving, I told my husband that I needed a few minutes with Sia by myself and then I would be right out.

I whispered in Sia's ear, "Jesus Christ is with you and inside of you. You're covered with the blood of Jesus Christ! The angels of the Lord encamp round about you! It's in Jesus Christ, Sia, that you live, move, and have your being! Jesus Christ will bring you out!"

As I leaned over to kiss her, I noticed an elderly nurse standing by who looked sad and said, "Most times they don't make it through this type of surgery!"

Now this was the last thing I was expecting to hear at a moment like this. It was almost as if she was Satan himself, but I looked at her face. Inside, I knew that she meant well, however, it was the wrong statement at the wrong time.

I thought to myself, "Miss, you'd better be glad my husband isn't in here!"

I looked at her and asked if she was a Christian, if she believed in Jesus Christ and if she loved Him?

"Yes, I am a Christian," she told me.

I asked her if she trusted Him and she said, "Yes, I do!"

I told her boldly, "With man this is impossible, but not with God. All things are possible with God! No-Thing is impossible with my Jesus!"[1]

I whispered in Sia's ear, "Baby, don't listen to what the nurse said. Keep your eyes on Jesus Christ! He's your Healer and the Author and Finisher of your Faith!"

I released the warring angels all around Sia to fight on her behalf! I began to declare Psalm 91 over Sia, putting her name in each area. When I finished

I kissed her and told her that I would meet her in the room assigned to her.

I did not doubt God although it looked as if all odds were against us. I knew in my heart He is faithful and would come through one way or another. We did not understand what was happening at the moment, or even why things were turning out the way it appeared during this time of our suddenly. We just knew that no matter what, God is faithful! Faith isn't hoping that God can, **faith is knowing** that God will!

I joined my husband and the others in the waiting room. We knew this was very hard for Pastor Sam. He'd been Sia's pastor for the past eleven years. Sia was eight years of age when we began our journey at The Gathering Place Worship Center. Now she was just a few weeks from turning twenty years old. This was the pastor she would always joke with concerning his BMW, (she would tell him that God said he was to bless her with his car), his response was, "I rebuke that in the name of Jesus!" Sia always informed Pastor Sam of her school grades knowing that he would reward her. He did the same for some of the other kids that attended church as well. My husband and I would always tell Pastor Sam that wasn't necessary and he didn't have to reward her.

Before we could get the word reward out of our mouths, somehow Sia would always interrupt by saying, "Ma, Daddy, Jesus is in the blessing business and Jesus wants Pastor Sam to bless me. Hallelujah! I receive the blessing in the name of Jesus! I worked hard for those A's. Thanks Pastor Sam! You're the best!"

My husband and I, Sia and Pastor Sam would just look at each other and burst out laughing! Because Sia was an honor roll student throughout school, she always racked up rewards from church and home! (Thanks Pastor). She also enjoyed his teachings and most times would jot down a few notes during his sermons. After service sometimes she would go up to him to let him know how on point he was during his sermons and also when the messages were a little lengthy! She always kept it real with him.

Sia was transferred to the neurosurgical unit at Halifax hospital where she was monitored very carefully due to the recent brain surgery. Josh and I met Sia there only to find every machine that one could think of attached to our precious Sia. This in itself was quite overwhelming.

As we began to observe the surroundings, we both felt as if we were in a daze although it was staring us right in the face. How could this be? How could a beautiful vibrant young girl, full of life and destiny be healthy one day and the very next day be fighting for her life? It's one thing to visit others in the hospital on life support, praying and believing God with the family for a miracle. However, there are no words to express your feelings and emotions when you are hit with the suddenly yourself.

At the very moment, Josh and I both felt so lost and helpless. I was reminded of Sia's adolescent years when she would come in the house crying because of a fall which sometimes left her with a scraped knee or elbow. Al and I would kiss and clean her boo boo and place a huge smiley face or super man band aid on the wound which always made things better. After a few hugs, kisses and a thank you, Sia would run off playing as if nothing ever happened. Al and I would be left feeling as if we had conquered the world. However, there are some wounds band aids just can't heal. There in the room lay our baby girl fighting for her life and there was nothing that her dad and I could do to make it better.

At that moment I was reminded of one of my favorite passages in the Bible, "People with their minds set on God, He keeps completely whole, steady on their feet, because they keep at it and don't quit. Depend on God and keep at it because in the Lord God you have a sure thing" (Isaiah 26:3-4).

III

How You Live in Private Will Help You During Your Suddenly!

*A*t home, we saturate our house with worship and prayer. I felt like we needed to create the same atmosphere in Sia's assigned room. Mother McDowell went to Target to purchase a Boom Box with CD player attached. We played William McDowell's "As We Worship" CD and a few other worship songs throughout the entire hospital stay. The next day one of the floor nurses came in the room to give us a CD entitled "He's Able" by Deitrick Haddon. She told us Holy Spirit instructed her to get the CD out of her car to bless us with. We worshipped the Lord night and day in Sia's hospital room. I even placed the headset earplugs inside of Sia's ears so the worship could saturate her entire being as she rested in the presence of God.

Three of Sia's close friends from Jr. High and High School, two College buddies from UNF, and a few family members began visiting Sunday afternoon. We knew many of them would be devastated seeing Sia in this state, especially since this was totally unexpected. Several of them had just talked with Sia Friday night by phone or on Facebook. Due to years of experience in the medical field, my husband knew that a persons hearing was the last to go.Therefore Josh and I encouraged everyone to try to be as positive as possible during the in room visits. When loved ones felt themselves becoming overly emotional, they stepped out into the hallway or family waiting room where they were consoled by Josh, myself, other family, friends, and even the hospital staff. Eventually we had to stop the visits outside of immediate family in order for Sia to rest.

Josh and I knew that we needed to keep our hearts and eyes on God in order to hear what He was saying through Holy Spirit. You can't hear clearly when fear is present. Fear comes to torment, cripple and paralyze you, but Father's perfect love casts out all fear! We needed to continuously encounter Father's perfect love. When facing a crisis like this, it's very easy to get caught up in all that you see and hear in the natural. Carrying the weight of other people's emotions, anxieties, and fears doesn't help matters at all.

I remember receiving several phone calls from people concerning Sia's condition. Some were panicking on the other end, while others tried suggesting which scriptures to read, what type of prayers to pray, etc. On one end of the phone I had panicking Lucy and the other end I had religious Sue! They both meant well, but there comes a time when you have to disconnect!

Finally I had to tell one person, "With all due respect, this is not the time to tell me what scriptures to read and what prayers to pray. If you want to be helpful, please just pray!"

Then I turned the phone off!

If we don't have the word of God in us when our suddenly occurs, the suddenly is not the time to try to quote scriptures to God. We will end up praying out of fear and not faith in God. The Bible says, "And without faith it is impossible to please God, because anyone who comes to Him must believe that He exists and that He rewards those who earnestly, deliberately on purpose seek Him" (Hebrews 11:6). We shouldn't just seek Him when we have a crisis. The people of God should purposely desire and pursue God everyday as a way of life! Trust me, my husband and I prayed every scripture that we knew and read almost every scripture from the Bible on healing. When we didn't know what to do, we just hummed like our grandparents use to do. Humming confuses the enemy every time. (The next time you are hit with a suddenly, I dare you to just hum!)

I also found out during our suddenly we needed to be still so that we could hear the voice of God! The scripture that comes to mind is Isaiah 30:15, "In quietness and trust is your strength." It's His voice that will carry you through every suddenly you will ever face. I guess I should give you a little warning, this type of response or behavior will cause you to be talked about. To others you will look quite foolish. Remember, each suddenly is different and will cause your response and reaction to be different. Your inner strength does not come from your pastor, mother, prayer team, family or friends. Don't get me wrong, we thank God for all of you! However, the victory is in one's pursuit of the person of Jesus Christ in the midst of the storm. We never want to get things twisted by giving others a place that only Jesus Christ is qualified and paid the ultimate price to occupy.

Although Sia was in a coma, I heard her voice speaking to me on the morning of June 20 around 3 a.m. as I stood at the side of her bed rubbing her face with my right hand. In turn I lifted her left hand and stroked my entire face with her slim fingers as I guided and held onto her hand. This, along with a back and feet rub, were things I would often do as we would talk after a long day!

As Sia's fingers continued to touch my skin I heard her whisper, "Mommy, it's okay, you can let me go!"

The voice was so clear and soft, it startled me. I looked around the room to see if my husband heard her voice, but he was sound asleep on the sleep sofa in Sia's room. I looked at the nurse outside of Sia's room in the glass booth monitoring the machines in Sia's room.

Then I heard again, "Mommy, really it's okay, you've got to let me go!"

I never opened my mouth as tears ran down my face, and then the third time very gently I heard,

"Mommy, it's okay, you did well, mommy, I'm okay because of you, you have to let me go!"

However, the fourth time was very loud and clear, "Mom, come on! It's not fair. You've got to let me go!"

The tone was as if she was saying, "Mom, come on, don't be so selfish, this is what you've prayed for all my life, that I would serve Jesus, that He would continue to draw me closer to Him, and that I would keep Him first. Mom you always prayed, 'Lord, don't let the things of this world lure my baby away from you; Jesus don't let the devil have my Baby. She's the only seed that I have to offer to you.'"

At that moment, I finally realized Sia was talking to me, I could actually hear her (spirit to spirit) and my verbal response to her was, "I can't, you're my only child, I trust God and I need you to trust Him, too."

I didn't hear her say anything else after my response. I didn't care who heard me talking or what they thought. I didn't whisper either. I not only wanted Sia to hear me. I also wanted every devil in hell that was listening to hear my response. I know I heard my daughter speaking to me just as clear as I'm typing words on this computer today.

Perhaps someone reading this book has experienced a similar encounter, but you were afraid to share it because of what others may say or think. I felt that way at first, but it didn't matter because I know what I heard. Father will tell you who you can share with. I also have a better understanding of 1st Corinthian 2:14, "The man without the Spirit does not accept the things that come from the Spirit of God, for they are foolishness to him, and he cannot understand them because they are spiritually discerned" (*Hebrew Greek Key Study Bible* NIV).

Later that afternoon I felt like I just needed some fresh air. I remember leaving Sia's room and getting on the elevator. After getting off, I began walking so fast I was almost running toward the exit doors. My two step-sons, Randal and Nayabu were sitting in the lobby area chatting. They noticed my anxious facial expression and stopped me to ask if I was okay. I told them I was but I just need to get some fresh air. As I exited the hospital, I noticed a palm tree in the parking lot away from everyone. With tears running down my face, I ran as fast as I could to the palm tree.

Have you ever felt like you just needed to get away from everyone and everything? That's how I felt. I just wanted to be alone with God!

Once I arrived under the palm tree with tears still running down my face, I said, "God, I need to talk to you! What is it God? What do you want? What do you want from me? God, I trust you, she's my only child. This is nothing for You to do. I have seen You do so many miracles!"

His response was, "Will you still love Me?"

My response, "Yes Lord, You know I'll still love You!"

His response, "Will you still serve Me?"

My response, "Yes Lord, You know I'm going to still serve You! Father, You said that You have plans for her life, that You were going to use her."

59

His response was, "I still have plans for her life and I'm still going to use her!"

"God, she's so young, she's was going off to Medical School. Father, I trust You, I believe Your Word!"

Holy Spirit's response was, "I never doubted your trusting Me, it's not about your trust, Paula. I already knew that you believed Me and trusted Me to heal her. I never doubted your trusting Me to heal Sia. I want to know will you trust Me enough to obey Me and let her go!"

I wept hard as I responded by saying, "God, it's so hard, she's my only child."

I felt like a part of my heart had just been ripped out because I knew what He was asking of me. He then told me to go back into the building.

I knew what was happening when Sia whispered to me in her hospital room on Monday morning at 3 a.m. "Mommy, it's okay you can let me go!" I knew Sia wasn't coming home the way she left Saturday, June 18, 2011. I knew that I would never hear her put her key in the door of our home again. I'd never see her come in from school, work or church looking nice while I was cooking.

I'd never hear myself saying, "Sia, you look so cute today, turn around for a minute baby. Uh, Sia, aren't those my earrings and necklace you have on?"

I'd never hear her cute laugh and response, "Hey, Ma."

I knew that Sia and I would never go get our pedicures done together again. I knew we'd never go to the beach, shopping, movies or even to the hair store to purchase our hair weave or hair wigs together. I knew we wouldn't go on family vacations or mission trips to Africa. I would never visit her in college for a weekend or even sit next to her in church. I'd never see her coming up to her dad and me after service giving us a kiss. I knew that life would be different for my husband and me without Sia physically being there. I also knew that I had to begin the process before it manifested in the natural.

On June 20th, 2011 around 6 a.m. I told my husband that I had to let her go.

He said, "I understand. I already did yesterday."

My response to him was, "I need to go home for a few moments just to begin the process."

When you receive a word from God, there will be times that you will have to act upon the word that was released to you immediately, even if it's not the word that you wanted to hear. It's His word that will carry you during the suddenly, no matter how painful the suddenly may be. You won't be able to share what God has spoken to you with everyone, some just won't understand! Truly it's okay and it doesn't mean they are bad people. What it does mean is that God loves you so much that He has chosen to let you in on or warn you ahead of time what's going to happen so that you won't panic or freak out. At the end you will still be standing strong for Jesus which in itself brings glory and honor to the Father.

Let us hold unswervingly to the hope we profess, for He who promised is faithful. (Hebrew 10:23 Hebrew Greek Key Study Bible NIV)

I contacted William McDowell's mother, better
known to me as Mother McDowell, to inform her of
what Holy Spirit spoke to my heart about Sia. Mother
McDowell came to the hospital to visit. During her
time there, my husband asked her to take me home
to begin the process of what I needed to do and
she agreed. When I arrived home I assured Mother
McDowell that I was okay and that I just needed a
few minutes alone. I told her I would call her when
I was ready to be picked up to return to the hospital.

I would like to clarify something. When I mentioned above that I had to let Sia go, what I meant is
in life there are times when our hand is still holding
on to a situation, although we've said over and over
again, that we have given it to God. My husband and
I came to the realization that no matter how much we
loved Sia, as her parents we had to take our hands
off of the situation and allow God to be God even
concerning our Sia. We had to let go totally and trust
that God's **Perfect Will** would be established concerning Sia's health! I believe this remains the same
for someone reading the book today. Maybe God is
telling you to take your hands off totally and allow
Him to move on your behalf.

When I put my key through the door of our
home, it was definitely different. *Wow!* I thought, *I
left home on June 18ᵗʰ with my child on the stretcher
of an ambulance and returned home on June 20ᵗʰ
by myself while my child was in intensive care with
every machine that anyone could ever imagine
hooked to her.* I began to open the blinds and walk
through each room. I looked at family pictures of Sia

on the walls as the tears ran down my face. I then entered Sia's bedroom, everything was left as if she would return. Homework assignments were checked off on her board. Her books, iPod, and computer lap top were on her bed.

I looked up to heaven and said, "God, Wow! This is so different! No matter what, I will still love You, I will worship You, and still serve You because You are my God. You are all that I have and You are so very faithful!"

After about an hour, I phoned Mother McDowell and informed her that I was ready to go back to the hospital.

On Tuesday morning June 21 around 5:00 a.m., I walked to the end of the hospital hallway to use the hospital computer to type out what Sia spoke to me on Monday morning at 3 a.m. and also what Holy Spirit spoke to me under the palm tree. I noticed that the hospital computer for families didn't have access to word perfect only the internet-email. So I figured I would type it on my e-mail, print it out, and put it in my Bible to read over and meditate on. As I began to open the e-mail, I heard Holy Spirit tell me to read Lee Grady's e-mail. I opened and read his e-mail which thanked me for praying for him concerning something.

My response was, "Lee, please pray for Sia. She's in intensive Care at Halifax hospital with a sudden acute brain hemorrhage."

Then all of sudden Holy Spirit took over and I typed, "Now I understand how Father must have felt when He saw His one and only Son Jesus Christ hanging on that cross, beaten to a state that He was unrecognizable. After all of the years of my being saved, attending church, listening to the messages about Calvary and the Cross, I now have a revelation of the pain that Father experienced. Yet the Father never allowed His emotions to get in the way of His purpose and His Plan, which was and still is salvation for whosoever will repent of their sins and receive His son Jesus Christ in their heart as Savior and Lord! The purpose and the plan was much bigger, far outweighed what He was looking at for that moment."

> *For our light and momentary troubles are achieving for us an eternal glory that far outweighs them all. So we fix our eyes not on what is seen, but what is unseen. For what is seen is temporary but what is unseen is eternal.* (2 Corinthians 4:17-18)

My question to Lee was, "What do you do when Father tells you that it's not about you trusting Him, when He says to you, 'I already know that you trust and believe Me to heal her, I want to know will you trust Me enough to obey Me and let her go!' Lee, a part of me wants to say yes and part of me wants to say no! Father is looking for a yes and I don't have that to give Him right now. Please pray for a Sista!

Shortly after e-mailing Lee, my husband came to the area that I was at and I shared with him what I shared with Lee, he began weeping saying, "Father, this isn't fair, take me instead of Sia. I'm much older;

she's just beginning. I thought You said You know the plan You have for Sia's life!"

My response with tears running down my face was, "He does."

I looked out of the eighth floor window down at the parked cars on the ground floor in the hospital parking lot. I was reminded of Isaiah 55:8, "My thoughts are nothing like your thoughts, says the Lord, And my ways are far beyond what you could imagine." I grabbed my husband with tears running down my face and held him and we wept together. I then told him that I had to let her go.

He said, "I'll go with you."

My response was, "Honey, I need to do this by myself!"

As I walked into Sia's hospital room, tears running down my face, looking at her lying there with all those tubes hooked up to her, and her face, eyes and lips swelling, I said, "Sia, hey, this is mommy, I love you so much, you're my only child, and this is one of the hardest things I've ever had to do in my entire life, but I'm going to honor what you asked of me. I'm going to let you go! I will not make a decision to pull the plug. If God wants you He has to take you His way, but I will let you go. I trust God with you, I gave you to Him after I found out you were in my womb and even after you came into the world. Before I ever held you in my arms I told the doctors to give you to your father so that he could lift you up before the Lord and that's what your dad did on July 15, 1991. All nineteen years eleven months of your life I gave you to Him. You've always belonged to Him and I trust Him and know that He will take excellent care of you."

I then turned and looked up to heaven with tears running down my face, holding on to Sia's hand with my right hand and my left hand lifted up to God and said, "Lord, I give you your YES! I let her go! I trust You with her and I know You will take great care of her. She was Yours from the beginning. Thank You for entrusting her to Al and me. I love you, Lord!"

I turned around to say something to Sia and was startled by this radiant glow on her face! "Oh my God, this is a miracle! Oh my God! Look at you, you are so beautiful, so radiant, and so peaceful, I haven't seen this peace on you since the day of the surgery, and the swelling has totally disappeared!"

I was blown completely away! By that time, my husband came in the room.

"Wow! Boom Boom, you are Glowing Girl! You are so beautiful!"

We both leaned over to kiss her and bumped our heads and started laughing. Shortly after, my husband stepped out of the room and I stood at the foot of her bed worshipping, and praying and just looking at her.

As I began talking to her, I realized, "Sia you're not even in there! This is just your body but you are not there! I could literally see this Huge being, standing behind me, feet never touching the floor, just hovering over me, hands out wide with a curve as if He were protecting or sheltering me, and he was wearing a Bright White Robe; then I saw Sia standing behind me, in front of Him, as I stood at the foot of her bed. I could hear her just weeping and weeping. It was as if she were saying, "Good-bye, Mommy," but also feeling our pain of her not being here physically with us anymore. I am not sure if it was Jesus or an angel sent to pick her up. I never turned around to look, but I could feel the peaceful presence of Holy Spirit. I could see them both. I could hear her weeping! Whoever this person was never spoke a Word.

Several hours later Sia was taken down for another test, and shortly after they brought her up to her room, the doctor called the family together. My husband, our sons Randal (Bas) and Nayabu, and me into the consultation room to let us know that she wasn't there, she was gone. They thought that Sia had just left, but in truth Sia had transitioned from earth to heaven the moment I let her go and told God I entrusted her to Him. On June 21, 2011 Sia Christine Yorker transitioned from earth to heaven.

So we fix our eyes not on what is seen, but on what is unseen. For what is seen is temporary but what is unseen is eternal. (2 Corinthians 4:18)

Four days after Sia's transition, I was relaxing in Sia's room at home with Biscuit who jumped on her bed with his toy, as he normally would do. I was lying at the bottom part of her bed and Biscuit was on the top. I began to play with Biscuit and all of a sudden, this deep sleep came over me. I looked at Biscuit and he was just sitting there looking straight ahead.

I said, "What are you looking at silly dog," and laid my head down on the pillow.

I was so sleepy, but I shook myself and sat up. I looked at Biscuit. He was looking straight up into the ceiling, his head going from side to side, but not making any noise.

I said, "Biscuit, what are you doing? What are you looking at and why are you looking up into the ceiling as if you are looking at something? What is wrong with you Biscuit?"

It was as if the dog was in some kind of trance.

Then all of a sudden, I said, "Oh my God, you are in this room, Sia you are in this room!"

I slid down in her bed like a mummy with my hands straight down by my side stiff as a board and tears running down my face. My husband was walking through the house calling my name looking for me. I'm thinking to myself, *how come he doesn't see me as he keeps walking by the room,* but I couldn't say anything!

I lay there with tears streaming down my face and whispered, "How come Biscuit can see you and I can't see you?"

All of a sudden I heard Sia say, "Yes mommy I'm in this room. Yes mommy Biscuit can see me, but I'm also in your heart. Mommy, do not stop telling people about Jesus! You have to keep telling them so they can come here!"

A thought came to me without me saying anything, "Come where?"

However, before I could even get it out of my mouth she says, "Mommy it is so incredible here, it is so amazing, it's nothing like you would have ever imagined! Mommy, it is so amazing! Mommy, I am sorry for all the times I acted as if I had an attitude with you, it is because of you that I am here! Mommy, thank you for all of your prayers and fasting and praying over me, and holding me accountable. You are the best mom in the whole wide world. I love you so much and I miss you so much. Mommy, tell Daddy I am so sorry! You just told me two weeks ago the importance of apologizing to others whether you're right or wrong. You said not to be prideful and act as if everything is okay without discussing your attitude concerning the matter because you never know what could happen to that person and you may never get that chance again. Mommy, tell Daddy he's the best daddy in the whole wide world and I love Him so much and I miss him."

I whispered, "I can't because he might not believe me!"

She responded very loudly, "Ma, you got to tell him, this is going to help him."

I whispered, "Okay, I will tell him."

Then I saw a quick flash of her step-brother Brock who had passed almost eight years ago in a motor-cycle accident, but before I could get the thought out to even ask, Sia said, "Yes, Mommy, he's here."

With excitement she said, "Jesus is here! It is so amazing!"

Then I saw a quick flash of her friend Sean's face, who was out at sea when her transition took place.

After I saw Sean's face Sia said, "Mommy, don't let him go! Mommy, you have to know without a doubt that he knows Jesus so he can come here. I want to visit with him but I can't because he's not ready yet."

By this time my husband finally came to the door and asked, "Where have you been?"

I whispered and gestured with my hands, "Come here, get down here, I have to tell you something!"

He asked, "Why are you whispering?"

"Shush! Sia's here, I didn't see her, Biscuit did, but I could hear her talking and this is what she said."

I began telling him all the things that she said. When I got to the part about him, he lost it.

He began sobbing and said, "I could hear her! I could actually hear her talking to me!"

So then I understood why she said, "This will help him."

"So it was you Boom Boom! Daddy could hear you!" Then he began talking just going on and on!

All of a sudden I heard Sia say, "Ma, daddy always goes on and on and on."

I burst out laughing. Quite naturally my husband wanted to know what I was laughing about so I told him what Sia said!

His response was, "I'll go on and on and on if I want to!"

I told him that we could only talk to her about things pertaining to the spirit, anything outside of that she wouldn't respond to because she is a spirit.

As I think back on this suddenly, it came to me that I might not have been here for my child because I had been scheduled to be in Abuja, Africa ministering at a women's conference. However, after prayer for guidance, I e-mailed the conference coordinator and thanked her so much for the invitation, but said that I would not be able to accept due to another service that Holy Spirit wanted me to attend. He wanted me to be in my co-worker's wedding because she had family members that were coming from Puerto Rico and they needed Jesus. He was going to use me to minister to them one on one. I was the only manager that she had asked to be in her wedding, no other employee from our corporation but me, and we were not even that close at the time. That's God! To be honest, I was quite shocked when He said, "Tell Abuja No! and Yes to the wedding!" I knew that I heard the voice of Holy Spirit and He had my best interest at heart. So I said yes to the local wedding and no to Abuja, Nigeria.

Do you know the day that I had the visitation from Sia in her room was the morning of my co-worker's wedding? That Saturday morning as I began to put on my Bridesmaid dress (that Sia took me to pick up) I began to weep because I would never see Sia with her wedding dress on or her husband and kids. Holy Spirit reminded me with a gentle whisper of her transition from earth to heaven. He said, "Sia's a beautiful Bride! Paula she's dressed in her beautiful wedding gown and dancing with the Best, My Son whom I'm well pleased with, Jesus Christ, the best Groom in the World!" All I could do was smile with Joy!

Before this suddenly my husband and I had received so many signs of the special fate the Lord had for Sia. Sia had been studying at the University of North Florida in Jacksonville. However, of her own desire and out the blue sky she called home stating that she wanted to come home for a semester because she missed her dad, the food, the dog, her bed and the house and me. Her comment was "Mom, I'm going to get a job and get accepted in the Medical Program in Gainesville". For six months prior to her transition, we were together as a family. She went to church, reconnected with her friends, opened up the new Ross Department store in Lake Mary, Florida, attended Seminole State Community College and was accepted in the Medical Program in Gainesville, Florida to start August 2011, two months after her suddenly.

When Sia was twelve years old, she was given a compact station wagon by an elderly couple, Mr. and Mrs. Black who were our next door neighbors. Mr. and Mrs. Black had known Sia since she was one year old. Prior to his death, Mr. Black told his wife who didn't drive much, that he would like for Sia to have their car. She would be getting her permit in a few years and this would be a great car for her to start out with. A few months later, Mr. Black passed and his wife honored his wish. Sia was so excited to have her own car at twelve years of age. Every day she would sit behind the steering wheel of the car which was parked in the garage with a big smile and the radio up loud singing at the top of her lungs acting as if she was driving. Sia was in her own little world as I sat on the passenger side singing with her and telling her to look out for the curve.

Several months later, Sia came to me and said, "Mommy, Holy Spirit said that I am to give my car away to Ms. Irene."

To be honest she truly caught me off guard, I wasn't expecting a twelve year old to make such a statement.

I said, "Honey, are you sure?"

She replied, "Mommy, Ms. Irene has been very faithful serving with us on the evangelism team. Rain or shine, she's always there bicycle and all."

I said, "You know what, you are absolutely right. I'd like for you to go and share this with your dad."

Sia told her dad exactly what she told me, a few minutes later my husband came to me and asked, "Did Sia talk to you about the car?"

When I told him she had, he said "Okay, no problem".

I told her how proud I was of her for sharing this with us and for having a heart to want to obey Holy Spirit.

I began to pray blessings over her and prophesied, "Because you are willing to sow your car into someone else's life, at the appointed time, God will bless you with a car."

Seven years later, just six months prior to her departure I received a call from a woman offering the church a car.

I told her, "I will contact my husband to see if there is anyone from our church that is in need of a car. Could you hold on for a moment while I gather paper and pen to take your contact information?"

In doing so, I heard Holy Spirit whisper, "That's Sia's car."

I stopped dead in my tracks and said, "What? Sia's car!"

His response was, "Remember seven years ago Sia gave her a car away and I promised her at the right time, I would bless her with a car?"

I said, "Yes."

He said, "Well, this is the time!"

I said, "Oh my goodness!"

I went to the phone and began to share the story with the woman on the other end!

She said, "I feel the presence of God. She can have the car."

When my husband came home, I shared with him the conversation that I had with the woman concerning the car. He contacted her husband and made arrangements to meet. A few hours later my husband arrived home with the title, deed, and a 2001 Silver Chrysler 300M, fully loaded, six-deck CD player, cassette tape player, black leather interior, sun roof top, and chrome rims.

When I saw the car I couldn't believe it! I thought to myself, *"Wow! God, this is so nice, Sia would not have ever received a car like this from us, not her first one!"* The car smelled brand new!

I asked my husband, "How much did they ask for the car?"

He said, "Nothing, they wouldn't take a dime."

All I could do was smile and say, "Thank You, Jesus, You are so faithful!"

A week before Christmas Sia came home from college, we never told her about the car. We hid the car in a neighbor's yard wanting to surprise Sia for Christmas. One morning while I was at work, Sia was on the computer looking at cars, she called her dad in the room with excitement to show him the car that she liked.

"Daddy! I saw a car like this last summer in black and it was off the chain."

He was speechless when he saw the car on the computer was the same exact car that the woman and her husband gave us, only a newer model. The car Sia showed her dad was a 1999 Chrysler 300M and the one that God blessed her with was a 2001 Chrysler 300M.

As her father regained his composure he said, "Yeah, that's a nice car, baby. If you want a car like this, you definitely have to get a job!"

On December 25, 2010 Sia was presented with the gift Holy Spirit promised her in 2003. I will never forget when Sia went in the garage and saw the car of her dream parked with a big red Christmas bow!

She screamed, fell to her knees crying and saying, "Oh My God! Thank You, Jesus! Jesus! Jesus!"

You would have thought she'd won five million dollars! She thanked her dad and me, but we told her we didn't do this. We reminded her of the car that Mr. and Mrs. Black blessed her with at the age of twelve, and how she had blessed Ms. Irene.

"Now God has kept His promise, the promise He made to you seven years ago. This is the appointed time and we didn't pay a dime for the car," we told her.

My husband and I told her the story of how the car came about and she just shook her head and said, "Jesus, I forgot about the car that You asked me to give away! You kept Your promise! Thank You so much!"

Sia also called the family that blessed her thanking them and letting them know that this was the car that she had always wanted. The woman and her husband were on the other end crying because they had obeyed God.

Sia is gone in the physical sense but still is around doing what she does best, instilling hope. Several of Sias's friends have left messages on Facebook or called about seeing Sia in their dreams. I'd like to share one in particular.

After Sia's transition, her best friend Dexter had a hard time dealing with her absence, especially since this was his first experience with death. Every place he went in Deltona reminded him of Sia, so he decided that he needed a new start and moved to Miami. Things were going well; however, he became depressed, lonely, began drinking and experimenting with drugs. This went on for several months, until one day he had a dream. In the dream, he was walking, and out of nowhere, Sia appeared next to him. She was talking to him but he couldn't hear her, but in his heart he knew what she said, "I'm still here with you, although you don't see me or hear my voice and I'm here to tell you that you need to get it together." At that moment, he understood that God allowed him to recognize how short life was and that tomorrow is not promised to anyone. He decided to return to Deltona, attend college, get a job and finally face the absence of his friend. On Sia's one year anniversary, Dexter was baptized at New Smyrna Beach. June 21, 2012, was the start of a new day; Dexter realized he had a purpose to fulfill.

IV

A Message of Love to Every Parent That Has Ever Lost a Child

*O*ur children are a gift from God. As parents we are to be good stewards over that which God has entrusted to us. Notice I said good stewards and not perfect stewards. A good steward acknowledges their inadequacy and unsuitability and will always be in need of God's help. On the other hand a perfect steward knows everything, has it all together, flawless, meets supreme standards, and therefore doesn't need God's help at all. We don't own our children. In case you forgot, your little Boe Boe or Mashella belongs to God. He lent them to you for a period of time better known as a season.

Our job is to love, encourage, nurture, lead, and train them in the ways of God through our daily lifestyle, so that our children in turn can reproduce, impact, and infect others with the love and person of Jesus Christ. Remember, we don't own them nor did we create them.

Train a child in the way he should go, and when he is old he will not turn from it. (Proverbs 22:6)

Wow! I just had a moment sitting in the library typing this book. To every parent that has lost a child, I want you to know that it's okay to have those moments of crying, reminiscing, and feeling sad. People can tell you that they know how you feel, but that's not true unless they are wearing your shoes. Notice I didn't say "have worn" your shoes. "Have worn your shoes" is what one would say after being passed up for a promotion, your husband walked out on you or the house deal fell through! The ache or even emptiness of the transition of a child is shoes that you will wear until the day Jesus Christ returns for His Bride! But it doesn't have to be downhill! You can live again!

However, you must be honest with where you are emotionally, how you are feeling and you must find a positive way to release your pain. Acknowledge if you are having a bad day, that you are missing your child, scream if you have to. I've had those days myself, I just don't keep all that grief and pain inside. You must deal with it and move forward. This is not a one-time deal. Trust me, you will have to do this on numerous occasions. I just want you to know that it is okay!

I've had many say they remember how painful it was when their dad or mother or cousin transitioned (passed away). With all due respect, no matter how close you were to your parents or other immediate family, there is still no comparison to the pain or should I say ache that one feels when your child transitions. No one knows how you feel better than God Himself! My husband and I miss Sia more than words can convey. I would give my legs or right hand to rub her back or her funny little toes or just to get a hug, hear her voice or to see her beautiful smile!

I would like to take a moment to share my heart with married couples that have lost children. Do not stop living! My husband and I recently celebrated our twenty-fifth wedding anniversary. We originally planned to renew our wedding vows, but it turned out to be a full-blown wedding, reception, and honeymoon. I wore the same wedding dress that I was married in twenty-five years ago. This was very special for me, especially since I had saved that dress for Sia.

Although your heart aches because you miss your precious child, continue to enjoy the beauty that God has placed around you. Most importantly communicate, express your feelings, listen to one another, and do not isolate yourself. Continue to be intimate with one another. Cry when you need to cry and remember to laugh! We are only here for a short period! God will help you through this!

As I sit in the Deltona Library weeping, typing, and listening to, "Always" by Danielle Munizzi, I realize the reason I had procrastinated in completing this book. I just did not want to go there! Someone may be asking go where? I didn't want to have to revisit the areas of the hospital, and all that took place. Although I do revisit those moments at times, it's on my terms. Writing God's book has forced me to go there more than I've desired. To be honest, I see the hand of God moving within, bringing inner healing to my mind, body, soul, and spirit. It's healthy to go there, just don't get stuck there!

After Sia's transition from earth to heaven, there were times when I actually felt as if I was the only person in the world that had ever experienced devastation like this.

One day I remember telling God, "The pain and ache is too deep, I don't want to live anymore, and I just want to be with you!"

I thought about my statement, and two days later I told God, "I changed my mind, I love life, and I want to fulfill the purposes that You have predestined for my life. I want to bring You glory and honor in the midst of the suddenly."

The truth of the matter is that I'm not the only one that has experienced the pain of losing a child. Mary Allen, a long time friend, experienced the same pain a few years ago. James, her only child went home to be with the Lord several years ago due to some health issues. James was in his thirties. I remember the day that I received her phone call informing me of James suddenly and asking me to pray for her baby. I immediately went to the hospital to visit James and to be there for my friend. Several days later James like Sia transitioned from earth to heaven. I like to think of the transition as a change of address. James and Sia moved from one location (earth) to a new location (heaven).

I can recall a month after Sia transitioned I took Biscuit to the park to run around. As I began walking in the park I looked towards heaven and began sobbing, I was missing my Sia really bad. This was the time of the evening that we would chat on the phone, she would tell me about her day at school or work, and of course she would want to know what I was doing and cooking for dinner. I walked and cried, walked and cried! I thought to myself, *Who could I call that would understand my pain?* I didn't need to hear she's in a better place, you have an angel watching over you or come on now don't cry, you have to be strong. The truth of the matter is I wasn't strong and I didn't want to be strong, I wanted to cry!

I heard a soft voice whisper, "Call Mary." I pulled out my cell and dialed her number. On the other end of the phone was the voice of my one friend that I knew would understand my pain.

Mary answered the phone and on the other end was broken, hurting Paula with one hand on my stomach, sobbing, and screaming so loud that I took the phone away from my ear. The cry of my womb continued for about ten minutes.

I remember wiping the tears from my face, put the phone back to my ear, and heard Mary's soft voice on the other end saying, "I know baby, I know, it's okay, I understand! God is with us! He will help us to get through this!"

I thanked her for being there and listening to my ache! She didn't panic and ask, "What's wrong

Paula?" She understood the sound of my cry! Sometimes we have to listen in order to hear the sound! Every cry has a different sound! We must listen to the sound in order to respond effectively or perhaps not at all.

Last year I was invited by a dear friend of mine, Pastor Chantel Wright, to minister at a conference in Harlem, New York that she was hosting. During my preparation for the conference, Holy Spirit instructed me to briefly include the suddenly with Sia in the sermon.

Before I could ask, "Where do I transition," Holy Spirit responded by saying, "Don't worry, just preach, I will transition." On Saturday, before the conference started, I noticed an older woman sitting at a table with two younger kids. What caught my eye was the bitterness I saw within her face. Although she was dressed very nicely, her eyes showed misery and pain.

Shortly after I saw the woman, the conference began and Holy Spirit did exactly what He said that He would do. After the conference, a luncheon was held in the banquet hall which I attended. I sat next to a young lady that sang beautiful worship songs to the Lord during the conference.

She and I began talking and then she shared, "You have no idea how God used you today. My aunt lost her son almost three years ago. Steve was her only child and she has not been able to move forward. I invited her to the conference. I was speechless when I saw her come through the door!"

As I sat there listening to the young lady, I heard Holy Spirit whisper, "Ask her which lady is her aunt?"

I asked and the songstress pointed to the lady that I spoke of previously with the two children. I sat there with tears in my eyes and thanked her for sharing. I went over to her aunt to thank her for coming. I asked her about the two kids she had with her. The question about the kids allowed her to open up and she began sharing about her son. The two kids were Steve's children, visiting for the weekend. She went on to tell me about his death three years ago due to a heart attack. I asked her why she was so bitter and angry.

She looked so puzzled and said, "You don't even know me, how did you know this about me?"

I told her, "The eye is the key to the heart. I could see it in your eyes before the conference began."

This grieving mother told me that she was angry with God for taking her son. She stopped singing in the church and with her Christian group. As a matter of fact she stopped attending church altogether.

Holy Spirit asked me to ask her, "Why have you become so bitter and angry towards your husband?"

When I did, she looked at me with tears in her eyes and said, "I don't know. Why did God have to take my Son?"

What I'm about to share with every reader is what I shared with this mother.

"I don't know why things happen, but what I do know is that God is the one that blessed us with our children in the first place. So many women desire to have children but for whatever reason are unable to conceive. He didn't have to allow us to keep our children for the period of time we had them, whether three hours, one month or thirty-three years but He did, and for that we should give Him praise! Who are we to turn our back on God with such hatred, bitterness, and resentment because the story didn't end the way we thought it should. He's still God and He loves us so much. He still has a plan, even in the midst of the suddenly!" Please start a new paragraph,

For those of you who have other children, lavish your love upon them. Don't neglect the others because of your loss and pain.

God could use the other children to help bring healing to you and the entire family. Remember, the siblings of your deceased child are hurting also. Come together as a family and share your grief, tears, and love. This in itself will bring the family closer. If you were left with grandchildren, you are super blessed. You have an extension of your child right before your eyes. Don't idolize your grandchildren or your biological children, just love and enjoy the time that you have with them. You will never get the time again. Cherish the moments for they will become memories!

Immediately a young lady around the age of twenty-five came over to me with tears in her eyes thanking me for sharing about Sia.

She went on to tell me, "One month ago, a twenty-one-year old boy from our church was killed trying to break up a fight. The church is having a hard time dealing with his death. You sharing today helped us, especially his mother."

As I began to ask her about the young man's mother, I saw a lady coming towards me, I knew in my heart this was the mother of that young boy. I came from behind the table, put my arms around her, and wept with her.

I told her that I was so sorry about her son and the mother held me tight as she sobbed saying, "I don't have any more children, Rashad is my only child."

Oh, my heart broke for this mother! I allowed her to share her heart with me! Rashad was playing basketball with some friends in Harlem. One of his friends and another young man exchanged some words and a fight broke out. Rashad tried to break up the fight, was stabbed in the neck, and passed away several days later. Rashad's mom and I spent a few minutes praying together.

I also shared with her about Steve's mom! Rashad's mom and I went over to Steve's mother, gave each other a group hug and prayed for her.

Before she left, Steve's mother came over to me to thank me for talking with her, for holding her accountable for her actions.

She said, "No one has ever talked to me the way that you did today, not even my pastor. You were straight to the point but yet so loving."

She asked Jesus to forgive her for being angry with Him.

She hugged me and whispered, "Pastor, this is the first time I have cried and hugged anyone in three years."

I responded, "Are you serious! You mean you didn't cry at Steve's funeral?"

Her response was, "No, today is the first time that I've cried. I need to go home and get things right with my husband."

Maybe someone reading the book has experienced the same type of anger and bitterness towards God because of your suddenly. Today is the day to make things right with God, your spouse, children, family members, pastors, and friends!

As long as you choose to continue to hold onto bitterness, unforgiveness, shame, guilt, and pain you are giving the suddenly permission to continue to control your life. The moment you say enough is enough and make a decision to forgive and let it go, you break all powers of darkness concerning that situation off of your life! It's time to deal with the suddenly, forgive and let it go! Forgiving others with a sincere and pure heart releases a true freedom from within. This accomplishment is obtained only through the precious Blood of Jesus Christ.

If you have not yet experienced an intimate personal relationship with Jesus Christ, today is the day of salvation. Please open up your heart to Jesus and pray this prayer:

Dear Jesus, I'm sorry for holding unforgiveness, bitterness, guilt and shame in my heart towards those that have hurt me. I also realized that I was angry with You because things didn't work out the way I had planned. Because of Your precious Blood that was shed for me on Calvary, today, I choose to forgive those that have wronged me. I ask you to forgive me for the wrong that I've done to others and for all of the sins that I have committed. I invite you Jesus

Christ, the Son of the Living God into my heart today as my Savior and my Lord. Thank you for forgiving me, loving me and for never giving up on me. Holy Spirit I thank you for revealing the person of Jesus Christ to me. Amen!

If you prayed that prayer from your heart, Jesus Christ lives inside of you. *Read your Bible daily to build your faith (Romans 10:17, Psalm 119:105), *Daily pray and get acquainted with God by talking with Him (Mathew 14:23) *Fellowship with other Believers (Hebrews 10:25, Psalm 133) *Witness for Jesus Christ Daily (Romans 1:6).

I want you to know that Heaven is rejoicing over you right now! Surrendering your heart to Jesus Christ is the most important and best decision that you will ever make in your life because it is a transforming and an eternal decision. I Love you and Welcome you into the Family of God! Please contact us to inform us of your decision for Christ! We would like to celebrate with you!

V

The Gift of Sia

"Sharing the Gift of Sia" by Dantrel Johnson

There comes a point in time when someone must leave their treasure behind as a legacy carving its impression amongst the young generation. Sia's suddenly did not seem true as each notification on Facebook indicated. I remember reading the many posts and long lists, and then quickly scrolling through my cell to text others about this! This was only two years ago, but I have given much thought to the "gap" between Sia and me before the critical point took control.

After the mission trip to the Dominican Republic in 2007, the bridge between Sia and me grew longer. We went on separate roads, in different directions. We were both in high school, attending rival schools, so we lost touch and did not see each other again until after high school graduation, three years later.

On the screen, the news looked unreal; the post captured my attention like nothing had ever before! It came during the same year I lost my great-grandmother and during the hottest season of all, when the "gap" between Sia and me finally collapsed. The RIP signs all over Facebook were the last place I wanted to see Sia's name! I quickly realized that God was trying to get my attention. Sia was only three months younger than I and less than one month away from turning twenty years old! The years seemed to have gone too fast, beginning when we first played together at Deltona Lakes Elementary School, and then on to middle school. During our childhood, Mrs. Yorker would always joke about Sia and I being a couple, although Sia and I knew that would not happen. We were both into music and kind of competitive about singing the old hits of the Back-Street Boys and N-SYNC. Then I can't remember being able to share our old experiences again.

Why did God have to take her? That first year I asked that question over and over again. However, I knew Sia really loved God. She lived for Him, and because of her strong parental support, I believe that she was able to travel more than any young person could, not only to have the experience of traveling, but to share the gift God had placed on her life.

I believe that her suddenly affected God's people in a positive way. Sia shined in all that she did. Her smile was one! As a beautiful child of God, Sia was an outreach to those with insecurities and low self-esteem.

During our mission trip together, Sia worked hard to comfort the little children in the Dominican Republic. Without her presence, without her hugs and smiles, the mission would not have been the success it was.

Sia's life light may have been blown out, but her eternal light is still shining today in my heart. It took me these two years to understand why someone we love is taken from us, but the recent passing of one of my friends' father has let me see that things are the way they are supposed to be. Sia had already accomplished so much in her short life. She had already done what she was supposed to do. "Many are the plans in a man's heart, but it is the Lord's purpose that prevails" (Proverbs 19:21 Hebrew Greek Key Study Bible). Her life may have seemed too short for some people. But in His timing His will be done. Thank you, angel in heaven.

"What You Do Now" by Randal Yorker

Okay, so really, what does one say when their little sister dies un-expectantly. Others have so many answers, but where I find most comforting, is that I remind myself not to put a question mark where there is a period.

Truthfully, I feel the loss of a sister, or any young person seems unfair. You kind of want to trade places so that they can continue their journey. There is absolutely nothing pretty about a young person in a casket. Your faith and religious convictions are challenged when confronted with the untimely demise of a young person. I attribute this to the forecasting of the individuals future as it develops, takes shape and begins to unfold before your eyes. There remains the expectation that they will achieve a prosperous future, create their own family and live out their dreams. Then, seemingly, the road ends for them and you ask yourself what happens to those dreams, all the effort expended, the investments made; what do you do now.

Well for me, after quite some review and revelations, I realized the road continues and never ends. All the dreams, effort expended and investments made become inspiration and a catalyst for your success. Her love and concern for others are demonstrative and evidence of a legacy for success as she had accomplished much and impacted many.

Now I know that dreams, effort, investments and character are needed in my travels. As I create my own legacy, I know for a certainty that the road may seemingly end but continues according to what you do now.

"Sia Christine" by Michelle Rosario

Being young, I've had the blessing of seeing more lives created than lost. Often at times I've found myself living more in the future than in the present, debating on which university to apply to, what my next job choice would be, or exactly how it is I would support myself through nursing school while living on my own. I got so wrapped around the "could be's" of life, trying to cross each bridge before it was made, that I completely forgot to take time and fully embrace the loved ones and moments that filled the present.

Sia' Christine Yorker's passing could not have come anymore suddenly than it did. Sia was not just a high school friend, she was one of my two lifetime friends. She was the bridesmaid years down the road that I knew would be standing at my wedding enthusiastically yelling "go ahead girl," with her bright beautiful smile. The one best friend that managed to give each and every one of my boyfriends "the talk" in attempts of making sure I never got hurt. Even more important Sia Christine was the one best friend I thought I'd grow old with.

Upon moving to Florida around the age of five, Sia was one of the very first friends I made in daycare. I always thanked her for our friendship because it was her outgoing vibrant personality that started it all. I was the shy, much quieter person at that age, but it was Sia's presence that always brought excitement to our friendship, and helped me strive out of my outer shell. Throughout the fourteen years of our friendship we shared hundreds, maybe even thousands of memories. I mean we even bought friendship rings from the local mall, got down on one knee and made promises that just like sisters we would never leave each other behind, that our friendship was forever lasting.

I remember the final days of her life like it was yesterday. I remember seeing the Facebook statuses of her being rushed to the hospital and wondering just how this could have happened to my best friend of all people. Sia was very healthy, petite, and always full of energy so even her illness became a suddenly to say the very least. About a couple of days in the hospital, I can recall what I like to call "the warning call." I received a call from Priscilla saying that Sia's condition was unchanged. I was speechless, didn't even know what to say. This was my second suddenly with Ms. Sia Christine Yorker. Millions of thoughts filled my head, how could this have happened?

I knew hundreds of people were making their prayers for her and she was so strong, I didn't want to accept the fact that Sia could possibly be passing. I cried and stayed in my room for the following few days. When people asked me of her progress I kept to myself, I just wasn't ready to face reality.

When I received the phone call of her passing I burst into tears. I couldn't even tell my parents until the following morning. I couldn't even begin to imagine what it could be like for Mr. and Mrs. Yorker after losing yet another child. I remember receiving that phone call from Sia on her thirteenth birthday when her older brother passed, being there for her, and hearing her tears through the phone.

When the day arrived for her wake, I went with my parents, a cousin who had driven from Tampa, and a past boyfriend. I stayed quiet the entire car ride. I had been to only two wakes at the time, but I had never been to one as lively and beautiful as Sia's. Sia was always vivacious and full of life, she was very outgoing, so I always knew she had a lot of friends, but her wake was filled with so many people touched by her life that I was honestly surprised we didn't exceed the fire safety capacity within that building.

Everyone took turns speaking on the microphone; friends, family, and even people who had only met Sia once. It was breathtaking to hear how she touched so many lives without even knowing it. She was definitely a pure soul. I remember Mr. Yorker asking if I would say something. However, I wasn't prepared. I was expecting a quiet wake. This was definitely different than what I was used to. The entire time I was there I tried building up the courage with my thoughts. I was so scared and nervous. What would I say? I couldn't just say anything, this was my best friend. She deserved words of perfection. Upset with myself, it was time to leave and I never said anything. My parents spoke on my behalf, but it was nothing like I would have said. For weeks beyond her funeral I beat myself up about it knowing that I not only disappointed myself but Mr. Yorker as well. I knew that if the roles had been reversed Sia would have been one of the first ones on the stage. I was filled with regret and really upset with myself more than anything.

On the day of her service I wore a sundress along with a bracelet Sia personally brought me back from Africa. The service was spectacular and somewhat set my heart at ease for the moment. In the middle of service and prayer, I began feeling weak, glanced up and started seeing white throughout the church. I held hands tighter in prayer, knowing what could possibly happen but insisting on making it through for my best friend. I thought it was the least I could do since I never spoke any words in her honor. I looked up again quickly after prayer and began seeing even more white and getting hot flashes. While everyone continued standing, I chose to sit down, not wanting to cause embarrassment or a scene. I knew I would have dropped to the floor if I had fought it out a little longer.

Towards the end of the service I began getting even sicker, "Why today?" I asked.

Out of any other day in the year, why this day, why one so important? By the end of the service I was sweating in a church that was cold. I asked my parents to take me home, upset that I would miss her burial, but knowing if I went on, all my symptoms would come to me passing out. I did not want Ms. Sia Christine looking down on that. As soon as I got home, I ate a quick snack, laid down, and my stomach virus began. It was horrible to say the least.

A year later, I was invited along with family and friends, to her one year balloon releasing memorial where her parents read a few verses from the Bible and exchanged a few words. At the end of the memorial, we all released the bright colored balloons in the sky. I had been preparing myself for this day for about a month. A month of dreams, nervousness, and depression that brought me back to a place I didn't want to be again, her death. I calmly walked out to her site and stood in the grass and prayed alongside of friends. I started getting really hot out of nowhere, sweating a little, and started to see white again.

I stood a little bit longer until I was reaching maximum capacity. I whispered in Priscilla's ear knowing she had seen me like this before and knowing she could help. I asked if she could help walk me to my car for my knees were getting weak. She asked if I wanted to say good-bye, and all I saw was my vision tunneling. I told her I would be back but just needed to get to my car, lay down, and grab some water. We "speed walked" to my car with urgency. I could hear Mrs. Yorker coming up behind us asking us to wait up, dropping everything that she was saying because she wanted to say good-bye to us. I was heartbroken wishing I could have said something back, but knowing I was far too weak, knees bent, about to hit the floor.

Priscilla feeling my increasing pressure weighing down her shoulder yelled to Mrs. Yorker, "She doesn't feel good."

I took two more steps and dropped to the gravel. I never made it to my car. A few friends rushed to me, placed me in a car, cranked up the AC, and laid me down. I didn't get it. I was fine. Why was this happening? Why was it that every event concerning Sia made me just a mess, physically? Mrs. Yorker asked if I was alright and if I had anything to eat earlier. I told her I just couldn't understand what was happening. One moment I was fine, the next I was getting heat flashes with my knees collapsing. In time I came back out, everyone staring. I was upset because this was Sia's day and I felt like I caused the attention to turn around. We closed the memorial with a prayer, hugs, and parted ways.

Throughout the years it has gotten easier. There are still times, of course, when I miss her. There are days where she is all I can think about, and nights where I want to call her. I speak to her from time to time throughout the day knowing that she can hear me and looks down at me laughing when I blast her song "So Sick" by NeYo in the car. I know she laughs because, well, I'm not the best singer and I'm certain if she was here she would have something to say. As time passes, Sia has become more of an inspiration to me. We shared similar dreams and I have made it my mission to fulfill my dreams not only for myself, but in her honor as well. I act in order to make her proud. Graduation Day, I know she will be there watching. She instilled fight within me, and taught me there is a greater purpose to life.

Being a part of her organization, "Sia Brain Awareness Foundation," has been one of the biggest blessings. It puts me at peace and allows me to continue her legacy, and do work in her honor. Her passing taught me to take advantage of loved ones around me, young and old because you never know when it is time for someone to go. It was like yesterday recalling our last shared moment, a "wifey" day at the beach, a gorgeous day in the sun with my two best friends. Then a few weeks down the road Sia transferred to heaven. Since then I have built a much stronger relationship not only with my family but hers as well. I am so honored to have the Yorkers back in my life for they are such beautiful people with inspiration and strong faith, who oftentimes remind of Sia themselves.

Down the road, I know Sia will be there, a seat will be saved at my bridesmaid table come the day of my wedding, as well as my graduation because that's exactly how it was supposed to be. Sia will always live in my heart. I could never imagine forgetting such an incredible person. She taught me many things in life, and those things will forever be carried within me. I love you Sia Christine Yorker and if you're looking down reading this, I hope you can know and feel even just a small fraction of the love for you I continue to carry. Even without being here physically, you have made such a difference in my life for the better, I can't wait for the moment to run into that beautiful soul once again where we can continue this friendship exactly where it left off. I hope one day I can inspire even a quarter of the people you inspired throughout your nineteen years of life and have a soul somewhat as breathtaking as yours. Rest in peace Sia Yorker, this one's for you. ♥

"How I dealt with the life altering situation that God allowed—My Suddenly" by Al Yorker

We will never fully understand the why's of God, nor the why's of life. I don't know what your "suddenly" in life may have been. Or if you have ever had a "suddenly" that totally wrecked your life, and had you at the point of giving up and throwing in the towel. I want to share with you about "my suddenly" and some of the trying times I went through, and how I found in God the strength to get through.

Early morning on June 18, 2011 began a span of time in my life that only by the grace of God I made it through. My daughter was air lifted to Halifax Hospital in Daytona Beach, Florida. When we arrived we were met with the news that Sia was in surgery. I could not believe what I had just heard. We were directed to the surgical waiting room praying every step of the way, that's all we knew to do. After what seemed like an eternity a doctor emerged, and when I saw him I knew there was something seriously wrong.

Shortly after speaking with the doctor, he told us we could see her, but also warned us of her condition and that she was on life support (a mechanical system to help her breath). When I arrived at Sia's room and saw her, "my life stopped." I could feel the blood run ice cold in my veins. I saw my "Boom Boom" (that's what I called her), lying there and there was nothing I could do to help her. I had always been there for her when she needed something. But at the moment when she needed me most there was absolutely nothing I could do. The only thing I knew was to pray and continue to pray and "trust God." We must trust God because He is all we have that will last forever. It's all we have that will bring us out of darkness into the light.

The next three days were the worse days I have ever had to walk through in my life. I don't think it can ever get any worse than this. My heart felt as if it had been broken into a thousand pieces. It felt like it had been ripped out of my chest. I had lost all desire to live. I wanted to die! And I told God as much.

I said, "Lord, why is this happening to Sia? Lord, she's so young, she is just beginning to live. Lord, put me in that bed, and stand her here with her Mom. Lord, raise her up. I know You can do it."

Then it started, anger rose up in me at God, "How could You allow this to happen, after You answered our prayer almost twenty years ago when we asked you for a daughter. What's up with this?"

I am not sure if I was angry because I didn't understand why this was happening, or because I didn't know what had caused this to happen to my beautiful lovely Sia. She had so much going for her at this point in her life. Her dreams, vision, and plans were now starting to come to pass. Sia had just been accepted into nursing school, something she really wanted and looked forward to becoming a pediatric doctor helping children. Sia had made plans to move into her apartment in Gainesville, Fl. She was so very excited about school and her future, and we were excited with and for her. We had just finished shopping a few days earlier for things to furnish her new apartment. We had planned to finish up the shopping the day this all started.

I am a very private person and I tend to keep things bottled up. Although I had many male friends around me, I didn't feel as if I had that one male person that could relate or understand what I was going through. My wife and I were there for each other for support and I thank God for her every day for being there. But you know there are times you just need to share your gut feelings with another man, man to man.

After Sia's transition I would go to the site of her resting place every day. This went on for little over a year. I would go and sit and cry and ask God why. God is so gracious. He allowed me to see visions and have conversation with her in the spirit realm but never did He answer the "why" question. I was at the site this one day and I was having a really rough day. I mean a really rough day as I blamed myself for all this. I was a retired nurse; I should have seen the signs.

"There must have been something I could have done."

Things seemed to be coming apart at the seams; there was a void at home. Sometimes I found it very difficult to talk about the void and how I was feeling, (all a trick of the enemy playing with my mind trying to get my focus and attention off God). I was sitting there just weeping and asking God to take me home. I just wanted to die. I had no desire to live. Then I heard deep down in the depths of my spirit man, "Look up, Look up!" When looked up I saw in a cloud the perfect image of Sia's face and she was looking down at me smiling.

I heard her say, "Dad, I'm okay. It's not your time yet, there is still much work that the Father has for you to do."

I will never forget that moment. A presence of peace came over me and to this day I cannot explain it. I don't know or understand why all this happened, but one thing I do know is God is real and true to His promise. He promises us that no matter what we go through He is there with us. He promises He will never leave us nor forsake us. He tells us to be strong and courageous, and not be terrified or discouraged, for the Lord our God will be with us wherever we go (see Joshua 1:9 Hebrew-Greek Key Study Bible).

I now go to her site on the twenty-first of each month (or whenever the urge hits) and spend a little time. This is a process that only God can walk me through. It has not been easy. But God has stood true to His promise. "For He has said I will never leave you nor forsake you" (Hebrews 13:5b English Standard Version).

Fellows, if you have lost a child or a loved one, trust God to walk you through all the pain. Trust God to dry all your tears. Trust God to strengthen you at your weakest point. Trust God because He will always be there. We as men have been taught that real men shouldn't cry. However, the aforementioned feelings are real and it's okay to cry and experience these feelings. Real men do cry. He sent us the comforter (Holy Spirit) to comfort us in the time of our most desperate need. As you read this my prayer is that you will be encouraged and strengthened by what I've shared, and know that there is a true and living God that loves you. I held on to this.

Even when I walk through the darkest valley,
I will not be afraid, for you are close beside me.
Your rod and your staff protect and comfort me.
(Psalm 23)

VI

A Message of God's Love to All My Readers

We have to learn how to get alone with God. Getting alone with God doesn't mean you have to be in a private place or location. Sometimes we may be in a surgical hospital waiting room with many people around. Some may have a relationship with Jesus and some may not. But as the people of God, we must get rid of all the hang ups and be willing to go within our hearts to connect with Father, spirit to Spirit whenever and wherever a suddenly occurs, regardless of who's there at the time. Remember, a suddenly doesn't happen at the most convenient time or place, that's why it's called a **suddenly**! It could happen while you're driving on the highway, standing in line at the grocery store, sitting in church, standing on your front porch talking to a neighbor, sitting in a board meeting or on a cruise with your spouse. Don't try to figure it out, just get alone with Father on the spot, go within, connect with Father spirit to Spirit, and allow Him to pour His love upon you as you worship Him in truth and spirit. This can only happen when you know Father intimately. Not that you have it altogether, but you're in love with Jesus Christ and you've surrendered all to Him!

Sometimes we say things and make promises to God due to a crisis. If you heal Aunt Susie, I promise to serve You the rest of my life. If You do this God, then I'll do that! The truth of the matter is, without a love relationship with Jesus and surrendering all, (that means Aunt Susie, our children, jobs, family, etc.) the words we speak are just words.

The word surrender means to give up control. It is an act of relinquishing control or possession to somebody or something. It is to give up in favor of another, especially voluntarily. It is to give over or resign (oneself) to something, as to an emotion. It is to submit to the power of another, especially after resisting. Basically it's just letting go completely, and allowing another to rule and reign!

When I invited Jesus Christ in my heart years ago, He was not just my Savior, my rescuer, deliverer, and one to save me from damnation. He was also my Lord which meant Paula was no longer in the driver's seat of her life. I handed over my life to Jesus Christ. I knew He could do a much better job with my life than I could. When I mentioned that I surrendered my life to Jesus Christ years ago, that's so true. But I also want you to know that I surrender my heart, marriage, children, family, ministry, areas that I serve in at church, and everything else in my life on a regular basis. Maybe you're wondering why in the world I would do such a thing. You probably thought once you invite Jesus in your heart, He's there!

True, however, you never want to think that you have God, Jesus Christ, and Holy Spirit all figured out. This leads to coldness, complacency, and staleness within your heart and relationship with Father, Jesus Christ, and Holy Spirit. Realize that you're not in control. Let go and allow Holy Spirit to be in charge of everything! You see, I never want to think it's about me, that I've arrived, no matter what comes up in my life or how Father chooses to use my life. I want to stay humble and broken before Him, because when it's all said and done, He's all that I have!

All that I am and all that I have belong to King Jesus, including my family, finances, and the gifts and talents that He's entrusted to me.

It is one thing to worship in a corporate setting on a Sunday morning when things are going good, but it's an entirely different story to worship and praise the same God that you say you love, adore, and live for when your life has been turned upside down!

I can't express this enough. No matter what you go through I want every reader to remember that God is faithful! His mercy (compassionate treatment) endures (carries on through, despite hardships) forever! God will carry you and me through any and every circumstance that we face if we will allow Him to do His job! One of the things that brings Father joy is when we put our confidence and trust totally in Him!

Holy Spirit reminded me of the times that my husband made some decisions that I definitely was unsure of how to handle or what to do, but I put my trust in my husband's decision, totally confident that whatever he decided would be the best for the family. This makes a husband feel respected and proud, (chest out but not in an arrogant way). He feels, Wow! She loves and respects me enough to know that I have her best interest at heart!

It's the same with our Heavenly Father! When Father sees that His sons and daughters trust Him even in the midst of the most tragic situation or within the simple day to day cares, this makes Him smile! We are saying, Daddy, I don't understand what's going on, but one thing I do know, You are Faithful and Trustworthy, You are all that I have, I run to You, rely on You, cling to You and rest in You.

There are no situations or suddenlies that you could ever face that should shake your love for God or your trust in Him. God is crazy about us, his love is so deep, and He will never give up on us.

Zephaniah 3:17 *The LORD your God is in your midst, a mighty one who will save; he will rejoice over you with gladness; he will quiet you by his love; he will exult over you with loud singing.*

VII

AFTERWORD

There were over 1000 people that attended Sia's home going celebration! Old people, young people, and people of all different nationalities came to celebrate. Many got saved! Praise God! Many that were out of church are back in church because of the suddenly that happened with Sia. Many marriages were healed, and many young people who hadn't spoken to their parents in years started getting things right with their parents and peers. Sometimes it takes a suddenly in one's life to change people's lives.

Recording artist Martha Munizzi said that she told her husband Danny when her time is up here on earth she wants a party just like Sia's! I told her I do, too! Holy Spirit was so precious! Father's presence was so real! Everything was so bright, colorful, and full of life. Balloons were everywhere. We asked everyone to wear bright colors, no black just bright colors which represent life! Sia was and is full of life. She's not dead, she's alive, and doing well with Jesus Christ!

As a result of Sia's transition, family and friends have come together to form the "Sia Brain Awareness Foundation" which began in 2011 in memory of Sia. Our mission is to educate and bring awareness of signs and symptoms of Acute Brain Hemorrhage or other brain conditions to the community. In addition, we want to encourage people to be proactive in taking preventive measures in avoiding head injuries as well as to console those that are experiencing pain and grief from the loss of a loved one due to a brain condition. One of the components of the Sia Brain Awareness Foundation is the Sia Yorker Medical Science Scholarship for High School Seniors. One of the goals of this foundation is to award scholarships to deserving Central Florida graduating high school seniors who will be full-time students in an accredited Florida college or university with an interest or intent of pursuing a Medical/Science course of study.

As of today the Foundation has awarded seven scholarships to deserving students within the Central Florida location. One of the first scholarships awarded was to the Lucille Wheatley Education Scholarship who in 2009 had awarded Sia a scholarship. Sia's heart's desire, once she graduated from Medical School, was to give back to those within her community that sowed into her life during her high school senior year. Although she transitioned before this could take place, the family and members of the Board of Sia's foundation honored her vision and desire.

Every March during Brain Awareness month, the Sia Brain Awareness Foundation holds a banquet to honor the recipients of the Sia Yorker Medical Science Scholarship. The guest speakers at this banquet include high level specialists in the field of Neuroscience. The Foundation has also been blessed with the opportunity to conduct brain awareness seminars in and through partnerships with United Parcel Service, and Dana's Brain Alliance, among others.

Among the many activities sponsored by the foundation is the yearly Brain Awareness Walk-A-Thon which is designed to increase awareness, bring the community together, raise funds for the scholarships. In February 2013 a visit to Accra, Ghana was sponsored by the foundation to educate the community on signs and symptoms of Brain Hemorrhage and other brain conditions on a live radio program.

The Brain Awareness campaign has also included Adopt a Street Program in Deltona, Florida, the United Way Volusia/Flagler County Reading Pal Program at Deltona Lakes Elementary (the school Sia attended), The House Next Door After-School Homework Club in Deland, Florida, and Brain Awareness Workshops in schools, colleges, nursing homes, churches, and businesses. We also distribute Christmas gifts to families in need.

We are rewarded in knowing that Sia's legacy inspires and continues to propel others to prosper and move forward. What comforts our hearts the most is that Jesus Christ is her Lord and Savior and to be absent from the body is to be present with the Lord.

If you would like to know more about the Sia Yorker Brain Awareness Foundation, we ask you to visit the website and please leave a comment. You can register to receive upcoming information or make a donation at: www.siabrainawarenessfoundation.org or call the foundation at 770-674-8120.

VIII

ABOUT THE AUTHOR

*P*aula Elizabeth Yorker is the proud wife of Mr. Albert T. Yorker and the mother of their Princess, Sia Christine Yorker. She is an ordained minister and founder of Yorker International Ministry, School of Evangelism (www.yimsoe.com) and Executive Director of Sia Brain Awareness Foundation (www.siabrainawarenessfoundation.org).

Paula holds an Associate of Theology, Bachelors in Pastoral Leadership and a Masters of Religious Arts.

Paula and her husband, Al, frequently lead one day brain awareness seminars and evangelism seminars throughout the United States and Internationally. She ministers, conducts mission trips, keynotes and speaks on evangelism, Holy Spirit, prayer, discipleship, inner healing, family and brain awareness. She has served as Keynote speaker at the Charisma Conference, and featured in Charisma Magazine and Spirit Led Woman.

Her ministry can be contacted at 770-674-8120

Lightning Source UK Ltd.
Milton Keynes UK
UKOW05f1845180314

228381UK00002B/39/P